ENDORSEMENTS

"This book is an utterly genius master class in connection, communication, and comfortable collaboration. You will find that as you are consciously reading it, there will be a comfortable room in your subconscious that is gently preparing for deep awareness to grow—quietly pondering, reflecting, and healing."

—Dipti Tait, Author of *Planet Grief*

"Finally, a book that synthesizes so many wise and wonderful modalities. Chaleff brilliantly pinpoints the most basic human emotions and conditioning, bringing awareness to how simple changes can make significant transformations. I have altered my own self-awareness as an authentic communicator through the insights in this book. It's a treasure and timeless. A book to be read over and over again."

—Gabriella Maui, Creator of *Dragon's Nest*

"Prepare to be moved, enlightened, and forever changed. Chaleff's unique blend of deeply personal anecdotes and razor-sharp insights serves as a poignant reminder that the art of building connections is a captivating dance between joy and discovery."

—**Chris Palmore, Author of**
The Mechanics of Gratitude

"Andy's brilliance is in finding an approach that applies to marriages, friendships, or even business associates. If you want to bring honesty and intimacy into your relationships and build lasting deep connections, then this book is a must-read."

—**Christopher Ancona, Author of**
The Alignment Quotient

"*The Connection Playbook* offers an abundance of practical ideas designed to promote strong, deep, and enriching relationships. Chaleff teaches us how to develop the required skills and inspires us to raise our level of awareness so that we can live with an open heart. Well done!"

—**Linda Bloom, LCSW, Co-Author of**
An End to Arguing: 101 Valuable
Lessons for All Relationships

"Chaleff's writing style embodies a perfect balance of warmth and intellectual rigor. The insights provided are not prescriptive or dogmatic, but rather offer a nuanced and holistic view of the intricacies of human connection. It is through this measured approach that the book resonates so deeply, providing readers with practical tools to navigate their relationships with grace and wisdom."

—Dr. Lynda Ulrich, Founder of
Goodness Exchange

"My partner and I listened to *The Connection Playbook*, and it saved our relationship. It got us talking and dealing with the real problems that were messing up our connection. If you're feeling unsure about your relationship, you should give this book a read. It might just be the thing that keeps you two together."

—Bambos Demetriou, Founder of
Unmask Photography

"*The Connection Playbook* is a hard-won, living document that contains the lessons Chaleff learned being an open and big-hearted man. This is an honest, direct, no-holes-barred exposition as to the work involved in establishing an attachment with 'the Other' and with your-SELF."

—Dr. Bob Deutsch, Founder and
President of Brain-Sells

"Through heartfelt storytelling, carefully crafted exercises, and practical advice, Andy has created a powerful roadmap to unlocking the untapped joy, meaning, and success that good relationships can offer us. Whether you long to strengthen existing bonds or embark on new ones, this book promises to be a wise and helpful guide on your journey."

—Frank Seisho Diaz, PhD,
Zen Buddhist Sensei

"I must confess that Andy Chaleff's latest work has been rather disconcerting, vividly highlighting my personal limitations in the realm of creating and maintaining connections. Without a doubt, this is one of the most comprehensive and advanced manuals I have encountered for establishing meaningful relationships. If there were criteria for the Nobel Peace Prize centered around fostering interpersonal understanding and harmony, Andy's work would undoubtedly set the gold standard."

—Peter Koenig, Founder of
The Moneywork

The Connection Playbook: A Practical Guide to Building Deep, Meaningful, Harmonious Relationships
by Andy Chaleff

© Copyright 2023 Andy Chaleff

ISBN 979-8-9885720-1-5

Published by

 Meaningful Relations

722 Sheridan St #138
Hollywood, FL 33020
www.meaningfulrelations.com

THE
CONNECTION
PLAYBOOK

A Practical Guide to Building Deep, Meaningful, Harmonious Relationships

ANDY CHALEFF

Meaningful
Relations

TABLE OF CONTENTS

Introduction 1

Section I: The Essential Conditions for Connection 7

Chapter 1: Relationship with SELF 9
  Exercise 1: The Wizard of Oz 17
  Pull back the curtains to reveal the source of your behavior.

Chapter 2: Trust Is a Must 19
  Exercise 2: Two Roads 27
  See clearly how lack of trust impacts relationships.

Chapter 3: Respect Is Given or Lost 29
  Exercise 3: Shut Down 34
  Reveal where there is disrespect in your relationship, and the consequences of it.

Chapter 4: Trust and Respect Together: The Salt
and Pepper of a Relationship 37
  Exercise 4: Lewis and Clark 43
  Map your most important relationships on where you stand with trust and respect.

Section II: Connection Killers 45

Chapter 5: Trigger Happy 47
  Exercise 5: Trigger Me Blind 57
  Dig into your triggers to understand what's causing them.

Chapter 6: Expectations Don't Listen 61
  Exercise 6: Check It Out 67
  Distinguish between observations and expectations in relationships.

Chapter 7: Assume at Your Own Risk.. 69

Exercise 7: Assume Away...73

Identify unspoken assumptions in communication.

Chapter 8: Giving Your Power Away with Codependency........ 76

Exercise 8: Stop the Madness...83

Reveal areas of codependence in order to take your power back.

Chapter 9: I'm Right, You're Wrong 86

Exercise 9: Truth or Dare...92

Replace defensiveness with curiosity.

Section III: Opening the Door to Connection............................. 95

Chapter 10: Personal Responsibility Is the Start........................ 97

Exercise 10: Lens of Love 104

View people through the lens of love rather than the lens of judgment.

Chapter 11: Loving Me to Love You.. 106

Exercise 11: 100% Self-Love... 111

Nurture deeper self-love within yourself.

Chapter 12: Repossessing Your Agency 114

Exercise 12: Popcorn Thoughts....................................... 121

Observe your thoughts without reacting to them.

Chapter 13: Personal Affront 124

Exercise 13: Label You... 131

See how you personalize and demonize in your communications.

Chapter 14: Impersonally Personal 133

Exercise 14: Five Steps Down.. 138

Open the door to deeper connection by becoming vulnerable.

Section IV: Creating Context for Deeper Connection............ 141

Chapter 15: The Energy of Intention Speaks Volumes 143
    Exercise 15: Pick Your Poison.. 148
    Analyze your intentions for speaking to gain greater consciousness.

Chapter 16: Influence Versus Manipulation 150
    Exercise 16: Four Doors... 154
    Let go of controlling others.

Chapter 17: The Why Before the What 156
    Exercise 17: Sort It Out..................................... 161
    Learn to set appropriate context for important conversations.

Chapter 18: Priming Mind 164
    Exercise 18: Prime Choice 186
    Learn how to prime people for important conversations.

Chapter 19: Letting Go to Get There.. 171
    Exercise 19: Lady Justice 177
    Balance your desire for specific outcomes with learning to let go.

Section V: Advanced Skills for Deepening Connection........ 179

Chapter 20: Listening without Prejudice...................................... 181
    Exercise 20: Hold Your Tongue.................................... 186
    Train yourself to hold your tongue when triggered.

Chapter 21: Ask Skillful Questions.. 188
    Exercise 21: Flip the Script 193
    Learn to ask more skillful questions that deepen connection.

**Chapter 22: The Process Is More Important
than the Content**... 195
    Exercise 22: Dig Deeper 200
    Deepen connection with deepening questions.

Chapter 23: Connect with Compassion...................................202

    Exercise 23: Four Dimensions......................................206

    Reflect on four dimensions of emotions to more clearly communicate intent.

Chapter 24: The Power of Touch......................................208

    Exercise 24: Eyes to the Soul..212

    Connect deeply with eye contact and touch.

Section VI: Navigating Tricky Connections...........................215

Chapter 25: Handling "Difficult Discussions"..........................217

    Exercise 25: Staring Down the Barrel.......................223

    Change your judgments to observations.

Chapter 26: Sorry Opportunities......................................226

    Exercise 26: Turn It Around..230

    Practice turning mistakes into opportunities for connection.

Chapter 27: Setting Healthy Boundaries......................................232

    Exercise 27: The Mirror Has Two Faces.......................238

    Turn negative, unhealthy boundaries into positive, healthy boundaries.

Chapter 28: Seeing through False Pretenses..........................240

    Exercise 28: Geiger Counter..244

    Become wiser at spotting manipulation.

Chapter 29: Loving from Afar......................................247

    Exercise 29: Present Conditions.................................251

    Identify conditions in your life that need to change to better honor yourself.

Chapter 30: Knowing When to Disconnect..............................253

    Exercise 30: Anchoring the Future.............................256

    Reflect on your final takeaways for transforming your relationships.

Closing...258

INTRODUCTION

LISTEN TO THE CHAPTER

At the age of ten, I struggled to read. My parents sent me to a reading teacher, hoping it might help. I was labeled "slow"—at least, compared to my two brothers, who seemed to have an easier time with it.

I was never diagnosed with dyslexia, but I still find it hard to sit and read. I feel an internal restlessness that never seems to dissipate. As a kid, I would bump my head against my pillow at night to wear myself out enough to fall asleep. This translated into struggles with my studies. I found it virtually impossible to memorize anything. I needed to understand things on a very fundamental level. Formulas were challenging for me because I could never suspend my need to understand and simply accept things without an explanation.

Because of this, I asked a lot of questions—so many that I often became annoying to my teachers. High school algebra was almost impossible. In response to my questions, the teacher once replied, "It's simply that way. Memorize it; don't try to figure it out."

This incessant need means that I have spent hours breaking things down into their most basic elements. As if untangling a ball of string, I learned how to slowly pull at each end until the ball eventually freed itself. Some of my greatest challenges and joys in life have come from taking something that appeared abstract from the outside and making it concrete.

For instance, when I learned Japanese, I spent years poring over kanji characters, trying to piece together how each symbol connected to the original Chinese character from which it was derived. Or when I learned to play the saxophone, I'd spend hour after hour playing scales until I could feel the notes in my body.

Yet what I've been most fascinated by in my life is the interaction between people. I have spent most of my life working out the "dos and don'ts" of human relationships. This was not really a passion but rather a means of survival.

As a child, I lived in constant fear of my father, always wondering, "When is he going to explode?" and, "Is there anything I can do to stop it?" I was hyper-focused on not doing anything to trigger him. It was nearly impossible. Little did I know then that it was completely beyond my control.

He was bipolar, a chemical imbalance for which he would sometimes take medication, other times not. When on medication, after a few months of relative calm he would say, "The pills make me feel dead inside." He would stop taking them, and then another period of rampage would begin. When he no longer felt dead inside, everyone else around him did.

At any moment of any day, with no provocation, I could be the object of his animosity. He screamed at me with such venom that it made no sense to me. He had no concept of or empathy for what he was doing to my mental state. As he often said, "The world revolves around me. Get used to it." I was held hostage by his mood swings.

Luckily, when I was ten years old, my parents divorced. It was a relief. After years of them yelling at each other, I was happy they separated. It meant spending most of the time with my mother and gaining an escape from my father's unpredictable wrath.

Only as an adult did I fully realize how much those years imprinted on and shaped me. The impact of being raised in constant fear—especially of a person who was supposed to protect me—is hard to explain. It's more of an unconscious state of readiness. A constantly buzzing brain that does not rest. Explaining this hyperawareness to someone who has not experienced it themselves is virtually impossible. It's not logical. It's beyond words.

What I learned much later is that children of an abusive parent, like myself, develop survival skills that translate into a high capacity for empathy. Many children of damaged parents may ask the same questions I have: "How can I hear the slightest nuance of judgment in a person's voice? How can I see someone's state of mind in a split second? How can I hear a single word and sense a person's pain point?" For most of us, this sensitivity is not a consciously developed skill but rather something that developed subconsciously for survival.

Throughout my life, this has been viewed as a talent by others, even a magical ability. But at the heart of it is that little boy who was forced to turn his entire body into a tuning fork, thereby learning to notice microexpressions on faces and subtle shifts in vocal patterns— to see subtle movements or a shift in the eyes.

I share this because this is not a typical how-to book with a logical, step-by-step formula. The insights, principles, and tools I share here came to me experientially. Only as an adult was I able to reverse engineer them to make sense of them. My invitation to you is to meet me in this experiential space and dig into the deeper knowing beyond logic.

This book is for beginners and experts alike. Everyone will get something out of it. I'd like to think that after you put this book down, you will feel as if you are wearing augmented reality glasses that give you a new ability to see and understand things that were once abstract ideas.

To create this understanding, I've broken the book into six sections:

Section I: The Essential Conditions for Connection

Section II: Connection Killers

Section III: Opening the Door to Connection

Section IV: Creating Context for Deepening Connection

Section V: Advanced Skills for Deepening Connection

Section VI: Navigating Tricky Connections

Each section builds on the next. I have approached this book for communications just like I approached learning algebra in high school, putting concepts into the simplest form in order to understand them. I've taken the seemingly abstract world of communications and created a guide map to deal with whatever the world throws at you.

An important part of this book are the exercises that come at the end of each chapter. These exercises are there to support your reflection and your integration of the topics in the book. Your best insights will come from applying the concepts by using the exercises. Even if you feel the urge to read quickly, I strongly suggest that you leave time for the lessons, or at least come back to them later.

Deep and fulfilling relationships are about finding heart connections. I will balance the formulas that I have developed over the years with the stories that make them come to life. Although structure may make something feel easier to understand, it also pushes us back into our heads. That might be helpful to some degree, but ultimately, head knowledge without heart understanding can actually lead to greater disconnection between people.

And that is precisely the purpose of this book: to help you create more connection between you and your loved ones, the people you work and associate with, and really anyone you interact with. I believe human connection is what we all want most. We all yearn to be seen, accepted, and loved. We all need to feel like we belong. We all want more cooperation, peace, and harmony in our closest relationships. All these core human needs are found in that space of connection we all seek.

The challenge is that there are virtually limitless ways by which we humans separate from one another. We focus on and magnify our differences. We refuse to listen to each other. We get hurt and put up emotional barriers and close off from others. We take things personally and misinterpret others. We project our own issues onto people so that we can't see them for who they really are. We can be incredibly selfish.

The even deeper challenge is that we often don't see these mechanisms that create disconnection and disharmony. In fact, we will often defend, justify, and rationalize them:

"He deserved it."

"I'm just giving her the same thing she's giving me."

"My parents made me this way."

If we can't see how we create barriers between ourselves and others, we have no way of dealing with those barriers.

Seeing and eliminating these barriers cannot come from a logical formula or process. They can only come from seeing ourselves clearly—our self-sabotaging patterns, the sources of our emotional triggers, our deepest needs and wants. It is not an outside-in process, where we learn specific tools and behaviors that will hopefully translate into greater consciousness and ultimately long-term behavior change. Rather, it's an inside-out process where we see ourselves more clearly, and that raised consciousness then naturally creates the behaviors that lead to deeper connection with others.

Love, compassion, and connection do not come from developed skills. Rather, they are our natural state when we remove the barriers that prevent us from living in that state. The quest to find them is not like climbing a mountain of accomplishment but rather like coming home to who we always have been.

I thank you for spending the next hours together with me.

SECTION 1

The Essential Conditions
for Connection

CHAPTER 1

Relationship with SELF

"I've wasted my life," she sobs. "I had an arranged marriage when I was nineteen. From the moment I stepped into his house, I knew it was the wrong decision."

It is now forty years later, and she plays a skipping record of regret. "He was a gambler. He stayed out most nights, and I raised the kids alone. I should have left him sooner. I left him once for six months and came back to him. How could I?"

"How are you?" I ask.

"I can't sleep," she says. "The second I lay down, my mind races with all the mistakes I've made in my life. All the missed opportunities. All the times I could have left him."

"And what do you see and feel come up inside yourself when you have those thoughts?" I ask.

"I feel regret and frustration with myself. I feel like I did not serve my children by staying with him."

I observe, "You mentioned that you left him many years ago, but it seems like he is still very much a part of your life."

"Yes, he is. I think about him constantly. His dishonesty and lack of concern for others. His mistreatment of our children. Him convincing me that I was crazy when I was not."

As she speaks, her tears soften, and her breathing slows. She pleads with me, "Andy, what do I do? How do I stop this?"

"I do not know if you can stop it," I respond, "and that may be part of the challenge. I know that you can make peace with it, and that will change how you experience it."

"How do I do that?"

I pause and consider before answering. "When I was a kid, I lived next to the 405 freeway in California, one of the busiest in the world. There was a constant buzzing as the traffic passed at all hours of the day. Eventually, I began to hear that white noise of the cars as silence. I remember the first time I reacquainted myself with silence. The quiet of my own thoughts was uncomfortable. And yet that was the space where I could begin to see the world more clearly."

"How does this relate to my sleep?" she asks.

"Well, think of it as a metaphor. Each car on the freeway represents a thought that is getting in the way of your destination. At the moment, you're stuck in heavy traffic on the 405, frustrated that you're not moving anywhere.

"When you go to sleep tonight, I want you to do something different. When a thought comes up, don't think about it; just observe it. Instead of sitting in your car, frustrated that you're not getting anywhere, observe each thought as it passes, as if it were a car on the freeway. If you have trouble observing, then allow yourself to observe that. Instead of your thought being 'My-ex-husband is terrible,' it becomes 'I see that I cannot let go of this thought.' What you will find is that by observing the thought, it becomes malleable, easier to play with. Conversely, the more you become your thoughts, the more you suffer—as you've already experienced."

This conversation with a friend is a process I'm very familiar with in myself. I have often felt like I am living with a schizophrenic brain—housing two people wanting two different things and never able to agree. I want to have a loving monogamous relationship, while at the same time, I want to have sex with some random woman on the street. I want to be alone but simultaneously want to be supported. In time, I gave up trying to make sense of these contradictions. I have made peace with this endless noise by learning that some things do not need to be understood, only witnessed.

It's in this murky world of frustration and contradiction that we begin our journey together. The world outside of ourselves only makes sense if we begin with what's happening on the inside.

When discussing communication, we generally think of two or more people interacting. However, if we truly want to improve our communication skills, relationships with others are the least important to focus on. The most important relationship we have is with the shadowy parts of our brains: the noise in the background that defines so much of how we react but of which we are utterly unaware.

This is what I refer to as the "SELF." I use all caps to point at a big idea that people have labeled in so many different ways: ego, personality, self-image, character, soul, spirit, etc.

The easiest way I've come to understand the all-caps SELF is in the balance between emotions and rationality. A thought comes up, and an emotion pops up right behind it. That emotion creates new thoughts, and the cycle continues. This quiet dance impacts all we do, and for most of us, it goes totally unseen.

This is obviously a drastic simplification. However, for the purposes of this book, it is more than adequate to help us address every problem that we will encounter in communicating. If we are unable to recognize the SELF, we are a byproduct of our environment. And if we cannot see our SELVES, it's hard, if not impossible, to change our behavior.

It took me most of my life to build a relationship with my SELF. It only started making real sense when I began to treat my SELF as someone else—sometimes two different people who don't get along. For our purposes, I will use a very simple diagram that you may have already seen.

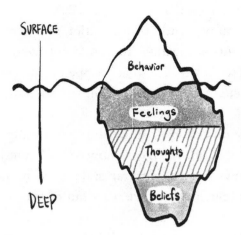

Behavior is like the tip of the iceberg that we see rising above the water. This is what we see when we look at someone. Thoughts and feelings are the bigger part of the iceberg that we can't see under the water. Behavior is tangible and observable: the words we use, the tone in our voice, nonverbal cues. In behavior, we see and recognize a person—or at least think we do.

However, if we only look at behavior, it's impossible to truly understand a person. Clearly, behavior comes from somewhere. How do we begin to see below the surface of the water? How do we begin to make space for the apparently unseen aspects of others?

In behavior, we have a peek into the emotions, either expressed or suppressed, which gives us a hint into why a person is behaving a certain way. It would be easy to stop there and say, "They are reacting to an emotion," which would be true, but that does not paint a complete picture. The next question is, "Why did that emotion arise in the first place?" The answer is actually very simple: because that person had a thought that triggered them.

If you look inside of yourself, you will see that there are some thoughts that trigger you. Public speaking, divorce, mother-in-law, death, children, father, mother. Now imagine that you are interacting with someone after having that thought. It will bleed into your interactions, whether you like it or not.

If I tossed you a ball, your natural response would be to catch it. The relationship between our thoughts and our emotions is just like me tossing you the ball. The ball is the thought, and your mind will grab, without even knowing that it has done so. Every thought we have has a corresponding emotion attached to it. Even if the emotion is no emotion, there is a connection between our thoughts and our emotional reactions to those thoughts.

For example, whenever I drive by a car accident, the thought of my mother, who was killed in a car accident, always comes to mind. Sadness arises. My behavior reflects this sadness, and I've often shut down emotionally. People around me will usually recognize my emotional shutdown but have a hard time tracing it back to where it came from. And since many people are like me and suppress these feelings, the shutdown creates havoc in relationships.

The core of this book is understanding how to manage our reactions to thoughts, first within ourselves and then in relationship with others. One of the questions I am most often asked, usually in desperation, is, "How do I change my thoughts?"

Answering that question is not cut and dried. In order to do so, we have to introduce a new word: "beliefs." Our beliefs completely define our lives, and yet we are almost always blind to them. An embedded belief system is like a magnet, pulling thoughts to us that validate our beliefs. We are so convinced of these beliefs that we call them "facts," carefully building arguments and curating our social circles to make sure that we are surrounded by people who hold similar beliefs. These beliefs define who we are. What we like and don't like. What we watch on TV. The people we spend time with.

When I'm coaching a client with self-worth issues, the unseen beliefs are often things like, "I'm not good enough" or, "I do not deserve this." These are not usually spoken out loud. They come from the quiet voice inside that is sabotaging this person's thinking.

Imagine that this person really wants to start an online business. He meets someone with self-confidence who has a thriving online business. The confident person tells him about a course he took. He thinks, "If I do that course, then I'll be able to start my business."

This thought will generate a range of emotions, from anxiety to excitement. The subsequent behavior is that he talks with friends and family, often looking for emotional support or validation. Imagine you're speaking to this person. He tells you he's excited about the course he's considering and how much it will do for him. You most likely only hear him talk about the course, not realizing that it's another way for him to avoid the discomfort of claiming his value.

We don't see this because we're not mind readers. Some very empathetic people may sense this, but it's not easy to hear what is not being said. What we can do is recognize that we are only observing behavior, and with delicacy and a bit of practice we can begin to sense the belief that created it.

Here is where it gets interesting. In order to understand where the belief is coming from in someone else, we must develop a deep relationship with our own SELVES. I often say that when I'm in conversation with another, I'm really listening not to the other person but rather to my SELF. I'm feeling where the other person's words resonate with my experience in the world. Keep in mind that in this space, there is no judgment of what the other is saying. It's purely about hearing my inner voice sense what the other is saying. Or stated another way, others are a mirror to my SELF.

I've had many people ask me, "How can you know so much about me, without knowing me?"

My answer is always the same: "It's not because I know you. It's because I know my SELF."

The SELF is almost never at rest. There is a struggle between the two forces of logic and emotion. There are things we think we need to do (logically) and the emotions that come up as a consequence of those things. If we slow down the reaction time between a thought and the emotional response—what is often referred to as a trigger—we begin to understand our SELVES better. This process does not work if we are placing a value judgment on ourselves or others we're observing.

To better understand how a behavior can be tracked back to a belief, consider the story of the arranged marriage that began this chapter. In it, we hear her judgment and frustration, and we also hear the belief that underlies it. She believes that she's not strong. She believes that she's not a good mother. She believes her ex-husband is an ass.

How does understanding this process help us? If we are unaware that we are driven by our beliefs, then we have no opportunity to investigate them. We have no opportunity to see that what we take for granted in our beliefs is actually not truth as such but rather a truth we have created for ourselves. Investigating our beliefs is not easy because those beliefs are very much part of who we are (identity), and questioning them has the potential to totally upend our lives. However, if we want to become great communicators and create more connection, we don't have a choice.

Digging into our beliefs is messy. One of the best ways to do so is to observe and become conscious of our triggers—the things we react to emotionally, as if in preprogrammed response. In these triggers, we can find the beliefs that are driving them without us even knowing it.

＊ ＊ ＊

Lesson: Make peace with your own thoughts first.

Behavior

Feelings

Thoughts

Beliefs

Exercise 1: The Wizard of Oz

In the Wizard of Oz exercise, you will answer a few questions to help you trace your behaviors back to your beliefs. I've given you a few sample responses to make it easier to start.

Behavior

Behavior: What do you notice about your physical state when you are reactive, angry, or sad?
(E.g., "My throat tightens." "I clench my fists." "I take deep breaths." "I cry.")

_____

_____

_____

Feelings

Feelings: What are the feelings that cause you to react this way?
(E.g., "I feel irritated." "I feel confused." "I feel angry." "I feel sad.")

_____

_____

_____

Thoughts

Thoughts: What are the thoughts that lead to these feelings?
(E.g., "He lied." "She's disrespectful." "It's unfair." "You only think of yourself.")

_____

_____

_____

Beliefs

Beliefs: What are the beliefs that lead to these thoughts?
(E.g., "People should be honest." "People should show respect for one another." "Good friends make time for one another.")

_____

_____

_____

When we are able to trace our reactions back to our thoughts, we are better prepared to consciously shift our behavior. As with the great and powerful Oz in the classic film *The Wizard of Oz*, once we see behind the curtain, our perspective changes immediately.

Our ability to see this in ourselves proves invaluable when it comes to making peace with our own thoughts and then translating that into our interactions with others.

CHAPTER 2

Trust Is a Must

"I have never fully trusted anyone my entire life. I haven't had that luxury," she tells me.

"Where does that come from?" I ask.

"My mother had mental problems, and she left when I was young. I ended up taking care of my brothers and sisters. The one person who I wanted to trust left when I needed her the most."

"How has that impacted your life?"

"I protect myself. Everyone has the potential to hurt me like my mother did, so I don't let them in. If I don't let them in, they can't hurt me," she replies.

"How has this shown up in your life?"

"I do my best to avoid situations where I need to trust or show weakness. This distrust inevitably sabotages the relationship because I am doing everything in my power to not be hurt. Better that I push you away than feel the pain of that loss."

When interacting with others or coaching people in relationships, the first and most important question I ask is, "Is there trust?"

Trust is vital because it establishes the basis for everything else in a relationship. In relationships with no trust, every interaction reflects that. Words are carefully selected to stay emotionally protected. Vague references to past experiences are made as justification to keep people at arm's length. "Remember the time when he did that?" "She always causes trouble." In an environment of distrust, there can be no deep connection. The less we trust another, the more disconnected we will feel from the other person.

This is certainly not to say that lack of trust is unwarranted. People spend years falling into negative patterns with family and friends. There are reasons why trust has eroded over the years. The question that rings strongest in my head is, "If there is no trust, then why are we discussing anything else?" Without trust, nothing else matters. You and your spouse could read dozens of relationship books full of great tools together, but if those tools don't address the fundamental lack of trust, they will ultimately fail.

We intuitively feel that loss or lack of trust as a giant wall in a relationship. Studies show that we actually turn off parts of our brains when interacting with people we don't trust—the parts that allow for empathy or openness to feedback, which are vital for healthy relationships. Think about that for a moment. When you do not trust another person, parts of your brain are literally shutting down.

One study used brain scans to analyze what they labeled as "in-group bias" to show how we treat people when we experience them "in" or "out" of our group. Researchers discovered that when people feel part of a group membership, it influences their brain activity. We instinctively distrust people outside of our group, whether that connection is based on family, community, nationality, race, ethnicity, or other factors. It sadly goes as far as a reduced sensitivity to watching people outside of our group experience pain.[1]

In another study, researchers discovered that we receive feedback from people we perceive to be in our groups vastly differently than we do from outsiders. They concluded that the mere presence of a person from an out-group can alter how the brain processes feedback, impairing it from receiving certain learning signals.[2] Simply put, we are wired to distrust people with whom we are unfamiliar.

When I read this study, a lightbulb went off in my head as I saw how I shield myself from those whom I do not trust. It was the exclamation to the point that if we do not trust, there is no reason to discuss anything else!

I am regularly asked by couples to coach them in their relationship. My answer is always the same: "Sure, if both of you are willing to admit that you've been the problem all along." By watching their responses to that question, I can tell how far along the relationship has fallen into distrust. If there is an unconscious shake of the head or a wince, then I know that the basis for my help—trust—is not present.

That's not to say that the couple won't be able to work things out. However, before we discuss what we believe the problems are, we have to determine if there is space to look at the core experiences, perceptions, and beliefs that have created distrust to begin with. Are they able to see beyond all the stories they've told themselves about the other?

Typically, what people are really looking for is someone on the outside to validate their beliefs. They want to feel seen and heard. When seeking outside counsel for support, it is often with the hope, "If they can't hear it from me, then maybe they'll understand it when it comes from a therapist."

What I have seen over and over is that once we've given up on our partner's ability to see us, we immediately fall into distrust. We use this distrust to protect ourselves. Therefore, it is almost always accompanied by blame: "I'm this way because of you." "If you just listened to me, it wouldn't need to be this way."

This is exactly why I've set trust as the foundation of all of my relationships and my primary focus before anything else. In my own life, if I feel that trust is even slightly eroding in a relationship, I address it immediately. The challenge is to recognize it soon and address it with love and compassion.

It happens quickly. An off-handed remark in jest can trigger a person without the other ever knowing it. There are many behavioral signals of distrust. People avoid eye contact. They don't meet you with a traditional warm greeting. They are quick to end the contact. The other person will most certainly feel that something is off but is unable to address it, which reinforces distrust. If left unaddressed for too long, the result is that many problems will arise in the relationship over time, even when neither party remembers what happened to create the distrust in the first place.

The dynamic of reinforcing distrust is common: Person A acts in distrust. Person B feels distrust. Person B acts in distrust. Person A feels distrust. This dynamic creates a negative reinforcing loop. A moment of discomfort in a conversation is internalized and begins to fester. Resentment grows. An innocent remark slowly turns into a breaking point in a relationship. In time, this loop of distrust solidifies and becomes stronger and stronger, invariably hitting a breaking point.

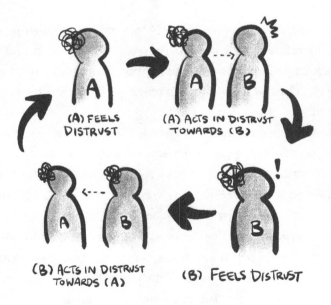

(A) FEELS DISTRUST

(A) ACTS IN DISTRUST TOWARDS (B)

(B) ACTS IN DISTRUST TOWARDS (A)

(B) FEELS DISTRUST

Unfortunately, people often seek outside support only at the point that distrust is so great that it's difficult, if not impossible, to shift. The stories have become so "true" that the individuals become stuck in their beliefs and pattern of blame and there is no way out; the only real option is separation.

The alternative ending to this story is addressing judgment, and the resulting distrust, in the moment. This takes a tremendous amount of self-awareness. But what is the alternative?

The irony is that the one who passes judgment is unknowingly separating in the relationship while blaming the other for the separation. Looking back at the systems diagram, we see that each of the behaviors reinforces the next. The challenge each of us faces lies in asking ourselves an incredibly painful question: "How is my behavior creating their behavior?" Or stated another way: "Can it be that they are acting in a distrustful manner because I am treating them in a distrustful manner?" This is nearly impossible for the one judging to recognize. The judgment, combined with the lack of self-awareness, is often the catalyst for a deteriorating relationship.

The reason for this is quite straightforward. At the moment we interpret another's words and get triggered, we are not giving the other person a chance to clarify and open the possibility for connection. Instead, we have decided to step out of the relationship. It happens so quickly that we're almost never aware of it.

A wife misinterprets her husband's words and gets triggered. She judges her husband and, in that judgment, separates from him. When her husband reacts to her judgment, she will feel the need to defend it, thus reinforcing it. They both dig in their heels to defend their judgments and reactions as the distrust grows and the disconnection widens.

Once we have projected a belief onto our partner (e.g., "He is lazy," "She's a liar," "He's heartless"), we now need to continually look for things that validate that view. The psychological term for this is "confirmation bias." If we believe our partner is lazy, then we listen to everything they say with a focus on where they are deluding themselves.

Here's a conversation I experienced with one such couple:

Her: "When is the last time you took out the trash?"
Him: "I did it yesterday."

Her: "Because I asked you to do it."

Him: "How about last week?"

Her: "Well, that was because we were cleaning the refrigerator together."

Him: "You never see what I do. You are always getting down on me."

Her: "You're not doing the things we have agreed to."

What we hear in this exchange is that the wife does not trust the husband. Imagine trying to support this couple. If a therapist says anything that does not validate her belief "He is lazy," he or she runs the risk of alienating the partner who is trying to make a point. We all face the challenge of the therapist: listening well to a person without taking sides, which would create distrust.

A question I have sat with much of my life is, "How can we help couples when the trust is gone in a relationship? Is it even possible?"

In TV dramas, we often see two characters fight and then afterward reconcile. The reconciliation almost always comes after one of the characters shares an experience so vulnerably that the other character is compelled to empathize. It becomes virtually impossible to project negatively on the other because they are baring their soul.

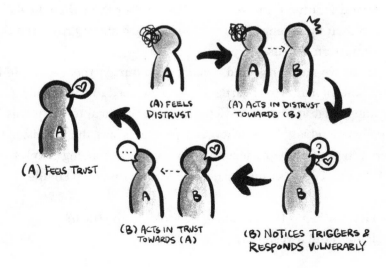

(A) FEELS DISTRUST

(A) ACTS IN DISTRUST TOWARDS (B)

(A) FEELS TRUST

(B) ACTS IN TRUST TOWARDS (A)

(B) NOTICES TRIGGERS & RESPONDS VULNERABLY

When we focus more on the things we have in common and less on our differences, we create an opportunity for increased empathy. From a place of empathy, it is much easier to approach difficult topics in a healthy and productive way. I can hear some readers saying, "Andy, that's much easier said than done." I don't want to imply that it is easy. But again, what is the alternative?

To make this concrete, let's take the same example above and see how the dynamic looks very different when the husband responds with empathy to the first cue that something is off, rather than reacting defensively.

Her: "When is the last time you took out the trash?"

Him: "Before I answer, can you tell me what makes you ask the question?"

Her: "Yes. You are not taking it out, and I am trying to make a point."

Him: "I am sorry that this is causing you frustration. I can see that I have been neglecting it the past few weeks because I have had a lot on my mind. It was not intentional. I'm just distracted."

Her: "Yes, I have seen that."

Him: "May I share a bit about what's going on?"

Her: "Okay."

Him: "I have not been feeling well. I did not want to say anything because I was hoping it would get better, but it has not. I see that in trying to take care of myself, I have let some things drop, and I should have told you, but I was scared."

Her: "I'm sorry. I didn't know."

In this interaction, we move from the symptom (the trash) to the source (the reason). Because one of the partners is able to find empathy, the other is moved to connect meaningfully. It's exactly in these moments, the ones that almost always turn into fights, where we have the biggest opportunity to connect.

We often look at the symptoms of people's behavior and ignore the source out of convenience: We don't need to understand or help them understand. We just want things the way we want them. And yet we want the same consideration in return.

In trusting relationships, we do not try to prove anyone wrong. We try to figure out what is not going well so that we can get even closer and have deeper trust.

✳ ✳ ✳

Lesson: Begin with "Where am I not trusting?"

Exercise 2: Two Roads

In this chapter, we discussed how a lack of trust bleeds into how we interact with others. It is not always easy to see this in ourselves. The following questions will help you see where you are in relationship to different people in your life.

Think of two people, one whom you trust and one not so much. On a scale of 1 to 10, 1 being "I completely distrust" and 10 being "I completely trust," how would you rank yourself in relation to each of these people?

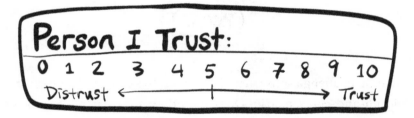

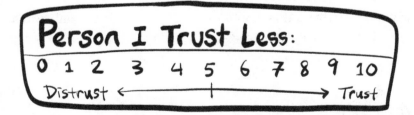

How do you treat these two people differently?

Person I trust: _____
_____
_____

Person I trust less:_____
_____
_____

If you were to treat the person you trust less similarly to the person you trust, how do you believe that might change this person's behavior with you?

It can be challenging to trust. Where did the distrust begin? It is a chicken-and-egg scenario. Does the other not trust me because I have never trusted them? Or is there something I have unknowingly done to create distrust? Finding that answer is not always easy. In order to work back to trust, we must start by giving trust. We must trust ourselves to be vulnerable without even knowing if the other will meet us there. It is emotionally risky, but it is the only way to test what is actually possible.

CHAPTER 3

Respect Is Given or Lost

"I am going to make partner in the firm in a few years," he says.

She rolls her eyes and retorts, "They have been telling you that for years. When will you see that they're just stringing you along? They don't care about you. They just don't want you to leave."

"That's not true," he defends. "Each one of them also had to prove their value. That's how it works. You put in the time, and then you get recognized for it."

"You don't know what you're talking about. They're just telling you what you want to hear, and you're buying it."

"That's not fair. I have worked hard to get into this position, and it's not all about being a partner. You don't know how it works. You've never run your own business."

"Apparently not. But it does not change the fact that you are deluding yourself. You will never make partnership. Face it."

This conversation, or some version of it, can flare up when two people have varying opinions around the same topic. It's one of the more challenging moments in a relationship because each side has a point. But for the purposes of connection, the point each person wants to make is irrelevant.

As stated in the previous chapter, beginning with trust is essential in any healthy business or personal relationship. But trust is not enough. There is a complement to trust that's also present in thriving relationships. If trust is the salt in a relationship, then respect would be the pepper.

Respect is an essential element—and not just a "nice to have"—because of the dynamic that is formed without it. If we look at the interaction that began this chapter, we see a lack of respect on both sides. Each party defends their opinion rather than inquiring into the other's opinion. Not surprisingly, in relationships that have a low level of respect, people are less likely to listen. They are less likely to be curious. And finally, they are less likely to value what the other has to say.

Respect is distinguishable from trust in that it has an active element. A presence emerges, and is seen, when people are showing respect. Their eyes are engaged. They ask questions. They concentrate to fully understand.

A good example of this dynamic is one I face with clients regularly. I'd refer to it as the "never good enough" archetype. I'll use an example of a wife looking to increase her skills through taking additional courses. The husband is frustrated because although the wife has taken several courses already, she has never translated that into making money.

The lack of respect looks like this: "My wife does not trust herself. She keeps turning to courses because she is too insecure. She doesn't think she's good enough, and that means I'll have to pay for more and more courses. And in the end, nothing is going to change."

In this relationship, how well do you think the husband listens to the wife? How likely is it that the wife feels heard? And what is the likelihood that this will turn into a fight?

The husband certainly loves his wife. He trusts her as a person, but he does not respect her or her process. Through one not respecting the other's process, a relationship falls into the negative reinforcing loop that we pointed out in the previous chapter.

A husband thinks he knows his wife so well that he no longer shows respect. In that lack of respect, which comes in many forms, the wife feels unseen and invalidated, which then turns into resentment. This resentment tends to eventually materialize into a fight-or-flight response. Either the wife yells and the fight begins, or she pulls away because she is not going to be heard anyway.

Respect is challenging in close relationships because we often lose it for good reason. We see things that our partner does not. Over time, it's easy for partners to see each other's unhealthy tendencies, weaknesses, and limitations. In a partnership, we have an uninvited historian at our side who remembers everything we've done or not done. The idea of the other person that develops can deteriorate our respect for them. As we watch our partner and judgments form in our heads, we are less likely to bring them forward because "we know how this ends."

The consequence is that the relationship becomes strained. The wife feels less and less comfortable sharing because she knows she will be judged. The husband has a story in his head about his wife, and she no longer has a partner in life but rather an unforgiving judge.

This dynamic turns into a very common argument:

Her: "I want to take a master yoga class next fall."

Him: "Aren't you a master already? You've done so many courses."

Her: "You're not listening to me. This course is going to allow me to teach."

Him: "That's what you said about the last course, and where are you now?"

The wife can often feel the frustration of the husband as abuse: "He is only looking to put me down." The challenge I see many couples facing, especially those who have been together a long time, is that they really do know their partner. Like many things in life, this is a double-edged sword.

If a couple has been together for decades, they may know each other better than they know themselves in many ways. A challenging question arises: "How do I allow myself to simultaneously see a person without prejudicing my past experience and not ignore my own experience?" Or put another way, "How do I show my partner respect through listening and, at the same time, respect through helping him or her see a behavioral pattern that he or she may be blind to?"

It's an incredible challenge and one that very few learn how to balance. Again, self-awareness is the prerequisite. If we are unaware of our own judgments, we will react to another without consciousness, like a Pavlovian response. A bell is rung, and the dog begins to salivate. Although the bell is the trigger for the response, the reaction is something that occurs inside of oneself. If we don't see how the bell is connected to our response, then we are quite literally our thoughts; we are not free to behave differently.

An alternative ending to the story above might look something like this:

Her: "I want to take a master yoga class next fall."

Him: "You've done a few classes like this already. What are you looking to get out of this one?"

Her: "I am building up my confidence to become an instructor, and this will help me do that."

Him: "I love that you are going for it. I know that getting more confidence has been a big reason for your taking these courses in the past. How do you see this helping in that regard?"

Her: "Well, charging for my services is uncomfortable. I see many others who have been doing yoga for much longer than me. I guess it will give me more credentials, and that feels important."

Him: "Anything that helps to build your confidence is worth investing in. I would love it if we set a goal that you deliver some courses yourself afterward. Can we have that be part of the intention, to make sure that we begin to create some work for you as well?"

Her: "I have a hard time saying yes to that now, but I will discuss it with you as I go through the course."

Although many will agree that the above conversation between the couple is preferable, the challenge is getting there. Respect is often lost in a relationship with neither party ever knowing how it disappeared. Most people are unaware of how to rekindle it themselves, and as a byproduct, the feelings that arise are turned into blame or shame.

In order to rebuild respect, we first have to realize that we have been disrespectful and acknowledge that the habitual behavior is not working for ourselves or for the relationship. In doing so, the judgment does not go away, but it's less likely to bleed into the unhealthy dynamic that, as we know, does not end well.

Our goal cannot be to pretend that we don't have judgment. Of course we have it. The issue arises when we bring it into our relationships. You will learn throughout this book how to channel judgment in more productive ways that actually bring people closer to you rather than pushing them away. It is possible to have judgment and remain respectful at the same time.

✳ ✳ ✳

Lesson: Respect is vital in connecting with others.

Exercise 3: Shut Down

It is easy to miss the moments where we are not showing respect in a relationship. The following exercise will help you better understand these moments and, more importantly, the consequences for your relationship. The exercise is populated with a few sample responses to make it easier to start.

What happens to your attention when you think you know what another person is going to say?

- I turn off.

- I get frustrated.

- I feel bored.

- I get tired.

- I lose all interest.

- I feel the need to interrupt.

- _____
  _____

- _____
  _____

How does this impact how you listen?

- I generally don't listen.

- I make a lot of assumptions.

- I nod, hoping I won't be asked any questions.

- I wait until I can speak.

- _____
  _____

- _____
  _____

- _____
  _____

How do you think that impacts the person you are with?

- They may notice.

- They may feel lonely in the relationship.

- They may feel unseen.

- They may get angry.

- They may feel the need to speak louder.

- _____
  _____

- _____
  _____

What will be the consequences of this if this occurs over a longer period of time?

- There will most likely be resentment.

- There will most likely be frustration.

- They will probably seek the company of others.

- We will most likely grow apart.

- _____
  _____

- _____
  _____

In looking at your answers, you may judge yourself or the other. Please do not. The intention of these questions is not to assign blame or try to justify anyone's actions. It is to witness how things are now so that you can heighten your awareness. Through this awareness, you have the opportunity to shift your behavior going forward.

When we listen to our partner with gratitude and appreciation, they will feel seen and heard. It's easier to be vulnerable. They even feel smarter. If we have the opportunity to create that for another, it's truly a gift in a relationship.

CHAPTER 4

Trust and Respect Together: The Salt and Pepper of a Relationship

Now that we've looked at trust and respect independently of one another, let's combine them. I present this graph in the hope that you experience yourself in each of the four quadrants. Think of this as a mirror to parts of yourself that you may not be fully aware of. As we walk through these quadrants, please picture yourself standing in each.

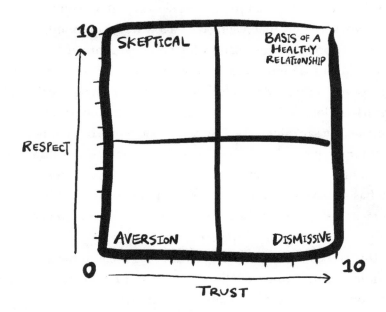

By placing "Trust" on the x-axis (horizontal) and "Respect" on the y-axis (vertical), we see an interesting picture emerge. In this graph, we quickly understand where an individual is sitting in relationship to another, and we can thereby anticipate the kind of challenges he or she will likely face in their relationship.

For instance, when we have high trust but low respect for another, we tend to be dismissive of what they are saying. We trust this person is good at heart and means well, but he or she doesn't have anything of real value to offer. When this person says something looking for confirmation, we might nod and ignore their excitement. This is exactly the dynamic we witnessed in the interaction between the husband whose wife was considering the yoga class. The husband loved and trusted his wife. He just did not respect that she could achieve the goal of making money through the courses.

If one or both people in a relationship sit too long in this quadrant, an undercurrent of tension and an increasing discomfort with vulnerability arises. Imagine talking to someone in this quadrant. How does it feel? How do you act? How easy is it for you to remain open? Now multiply that feeling over a few weeks or months. What is the likelihood that this relationship is going to thrive?

If we instead jump to the opposite corner, with low trust but high respect, we see different feelings emerge. We recognize that this person has a lot to offer, but we don't feel safe with him or her. We are skeptical. We say things like, "He does good work, but I'm not sure about him in general." Or, "He's smart, but I don't feel comfortable around him." What feelings come up when you are with someone who has achieved a lot and yet you don't trust them? How safe is this relationship? For some, feelings of aggression and aversion can emerge, while others will experience fear.

This is why both of these qualities are essential for a healthy relationship. And when relationships are out of balance in either direction, it is reflected in all our interactions.

If we are in the lower left quadrant, this relationship is in serious distress and is most likely highly reactive, with both parties either fighting or running away. If you want to understand this quadrant better, think of anyone in your life who has gone through a bitter divorce. There is neither trust nor respect, which turns into a painful and costly lesson for both. The label in this quadrant is aversion for good reason. Here is where we go as far as paying lawyers so that we don't even need to face one another. Thankfully, knowing where we are in this graph is the first step to shifting behavior.

My wife, Rani, and I have been in all these quadrants at one point or another during our relationship. When we started off, we didn't understand exactly what to expect from each other. In that dating phase before calling ourselves "boyfriend and girlfriend," she made comments that she did not want to move too quickly.

"We should not push for exclusivity," she said.

Since I was ready to be more serious, her comments made my trust in the relationship low. Although I respected her decision, I was cautious. I couldn't help but notice her receiving text messages when we were together. I got triggered when I saw her look and appear to keep it secret. In this phase of our relationship, I was never quite sure where we stood. Of course, this lack of trust translated into our interactions.

This all came to a head one morning when she informed me casually that she was technically still married.

"I have to get through a divorce," she said.

"What?!" I exclaimed. "Are you kidding?"

"No," she responded. "I'm still married, and I need to finalize my divorce."

"Don't you think you should have told me this at the very beginning?" I asked.

"No," she said. "It doesn't affect our relationship, so why would it matter? It's not relevant to you."

"Hold on," I replied. "You don't get to decide what is relevant for me. If you think something isn't relevant for me, then please ask. Don't assume. Please let me be the judge of what I do not find relevant."

The lack of trust that had built up over time had a moment to release. We moved through it and eventually on to a deeper level of trust, but it took a few months to understand what was important for the other.

We've now been together for more than fifteen years. There have been many times when our dynamic flipped to the other quadrants, where I had high trust for Rani but showed low levels of respect. In our first years together, a common discussion arose. She would share stories of problems she encountered at work, and I would immediately offer solutions. I was not respecting her, nor was I caring for her needs. By always coming back with solutions, I was dismissing the very real possibility that she had already considered what I was suggesting. And I almost never asked for permission.

I've learned since that when I feel I have a solution for someone's issue, I should first ask permission to share. Even if a person appears to ask for it, I still check. Now a typical talk with Rani looks something like this:

Her: "I am having some challenges at work. I'd like to know what you think."

Me: "Okay. Is it okay for me to interrupt you when I have a question?"

Her: "No, please wait until the end. I'm trying to work this out, and it helps when you listen."

Me: "Okay, so you are not really looking for me to comment."

Her: "I can't say that yet. If I see that I am unable to work this out by speaking it out loud, then I'd appreciate your recommendations."

When Rani asks me for support, I do not even assume that she wants my thoughts on the matter. I respect her process, and as long as she decides how she'd like me to be present for her, I can do that. It was not always like this. In our early years, conversations would go something like this:

Her: "So, I am having a problem at work with Billy, and I think I should—"

Me: "Before you say another word, why don't you simply get rid of him? You've been discussing this for a long time, and I don't see it going anywhere."

Her: "This isn't really helping."

Me: "Maybe so, but you asked me for my opinion, and I am giving it to you."

Her: "I did not want your opinion. I wanted your support."

Me: "Well, this is what my support looks like."

I was not respecting Rani because I had already judged that she was not dealing with the situation well. I saw things that I thought she should be doing, without really understanding the context of what she faced. Lack of respect shows up when we no longer are curious about how the situation may unfold because we already have so many preconceived ideas of how it should be dealt with.

In our relationship today, we very infrequently fall into the top left or bottom right quadrants. When it does occur, we are quick to discuss it. There is no lag time between the discomfort and the inevitable discussion. This is where a lot of damage occurs in relationships: the hours of festering thoughts that then bleed into the discussion afterward. The emotional buildup has the potential to turn into an explosion.

I often say, "We are always one day away from a divorce." It sounds callous, but I mean it genuinely and with clear intention. I have never really liked the wedding vow "I take you to be my lawfully wedded [husband/wife], to have and to hold, from this day forward, for better, for worse, for richer, for poorer, in sickness and in health, until death do us part." I have found that it can be an excuse to avoid difficult but necessary discussions that may very well lead to divorce.

This leads to an interesting paradox. In wanting to avoid a divorce by not discussing the difficult things, there is a higher likelihood of ending up with one—because if we don't discuss the hard things, our relationships grow weighted down with everything that's undealt with. I proclaim that we are always a day away from a divorce as a way of making sure that nothing goes unsaid. It ensures that we never take our relationship for granted. In that way, we don't rest in complacency. We don't accept the narrative that life is suffering at the hands of the other just because we agreed to it at an altar. My preference is to love Rani more each year—and so far, so good. But we are still always one day away from a divorce.

As you dance between these quadrants, realize that there is a great likelihood that the other is in the same quadrant in relationship to you. Very rarely do we distrust someone who trusts us. Going back to the systems diagram, by treating someone a certain way, we engender in them the same feeling in relation to us, and the state of distrust reinforces itself. We do both of us a favor by sharing how we are feeling, without judgment or expectations, as a way of creating a new level of trust and respect. We will get to how to do that later in this book.

Lesson: If trust or respect has been lost, start there.

Exercise 4: Lewis and Clark

In this chapter, we learned the importance of balancing trust and respect. In this exercise, just as Lewis and Clark mapped their exploration across the Continental Divide of the Americas in the early 1800s, so too will you map some of your most important relationships. Take three people in your life with whom you have varied relationships. Run through the following questions for each of the three people you have chosen and put a dot where they land on the graph.

- **On a scale from 1 to 10 (1 being not at all and 10 being completely), how far do I trust this person?**

- **On a scale from 1 to 10, how far do I respect this person?**

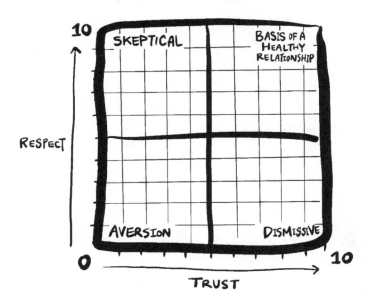

Reflecting on your answers will help you see where you are in relation to these people in your life. Take a moment to see where you placed your marks. If your marks are either in the top left or bottom right quadrants, there are things you can do to improve the relationship. If you are in the bottom left, the journey will be a bit tougher.

In the end, this is a decision we get to make. But we must keep in mind that there are consequences for our mental and physical well-being that go well beyond our relationships. This leads to a conclusion I have drawn for myself: I heal my troubled relationships not for others but rather for myself.

People often have a hard time dedicating to healing a broken relationship because the odds can feel insurmountable. I like to look at it another way. What is the cost of not healing the relationship? What are the chances that this relationship will flourish if I give up on it?

SECTION II

Connection Killers

CHAPTER 5

Trigger Happy

"What do you want?" my father demanded.

I was thirteen years old, and we were sitting at our round dining room table. It was a scary question for me because he was very insistent on an answer, and I was afraid of answering it incorrectly and triggering him.

In a moment of complete surrender, I told him in a soft voice what I really wanted. "I want you to be more like Jimmy Roger's dad."

He flipped. His eyes filled with rage. He yelled with such intensity that the walls shook. He grabbed me by the back of my neck and tossed me out of the house, screaming at the top of his lungs. I walked to my mother's house, crying in the dark.

As we navigate life, we encounter situations that snap us into a reactive state. We're going about our day, someone says something, and *BANG!* Our heart rate and temperature rise. The tone of our voice changes. We feel defensive.

Although these triggers are different for everyone, their impact is the same. We turn into a very different person. The *Strange Case of Dr. Jekyll and Mr. Hyde* comes to mind. Except, in our case, the change happens not with a potion but rather with a set of words or a situation. If we're not conscious of what lies behind our triggers, we can turn into the very people we try our best not to be, which is almost always followed with regret.

Triggers are generally connected with judgments, expectations, and blind beliefs. A trigger is this magical gift that tells you, "Here you go; this is something you get to work on."

If we choose to ignore our triggers and simply react to them, we will experience the same patterns over and over again in our lives, with no awareness of what's happening or why. It's easier to see these patterns in others. But in the end, I guarantee you one thing. There is a commonality in all your failed relationships: it is—drumroll—you.

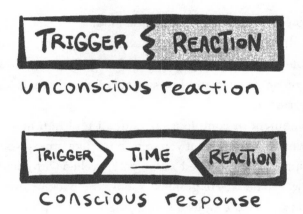

Certain people and situations will trigger us predictably, and we have no choice over whether we engage with that trigger or not. In such an automatic response, it's hard to even know that we are reacting until it is too late. To defend our reactions, we have a story around the trigger that is so watertight in our minds that anyone who disagrees with us is seen as ignorant, dangerous, or abusive— any label that denigrates them so we can remain comfortable in our triggers. "It's her fault." "He is gaslighting me." "She is psycho."

People who don't take responsibility for their triggers can be dogmatic in their thinking and, in a strange and twisted way, blame others for the way those others make them feel. In today's society, we have even created code phrases so that people can blame someone else for their discomfort: "I don't feel safe"; "He is a narcissist"; "You are being aggressive."

It's essential to remember that trying to have logical discussions with someone while they are triggered is futile. This is clearly a challenge because not being triggered by a person who is triggered takes some self-awareness. We need only go back to the systems diagram to understand what happens when two triggered people are interacting.

I state this emphatically not only because of my experience but also because of human understanding of the brain. When someone is triggered, their amygdala, which is tied to our fight, flight, or freeze response, is activated. This reptilian part of our brains is all about survival and blocks our access to the neocortex and our higher-level thinking. In those moments of trigger, we are talking not to the reserved Mr. Hyde version of our partner but rather to the Dr. Jekyll. And if you have read the book by Robert Louis Stevenson, you'll know that it does not end well for those interacting with him.

Triggers are our Achilles' heel. They disrupt our lives and ruin opportunities for connection. Until we find a way to make peace with our triggers and respond consciously to them, they define our lives. A trigger is like a box we place ourselves into. If we have no awareness of it or control over it, we stay stuck inside that box, limited by our predictable reactions. Thankfully, triggers give us the opportunity for some incredible self-discovery.

I've shared how I was terrified of my father as a child. Obviously, that experience created a lot of triggers for me as an adult. For example, I built a belief around anger that created a massive recurring trigger for me. If I was around someone who displayed any anger, I immediately deemed them unsafe. I judged them as underdeveloped, disrespectful, and dangerous.

This belief impacted me in many ways that I was unaware of. First of all, there was no space to discuss it. If anyone brought up the subject of anger, I would tell my story and discount whatever they had to say. Whenever they presented a valid or valuable point, I would immediately fall into defense and blame the other for their shortsightedness. This was an uncomfortable place to be, and I was unable to see that my belief was holding me there. I treated the idea that anger is categorically bad as an incontrovertible "truth."

In my life, this translated into judgment, not only of others but also of myself. Whenever we are unable to make peace with the emotions inside us, we begin to point at and judge those emotions in others. Whenever I felt a hint of anger, I immediately repressed it. I'd feel it arise deep in my belly, and the struggle would begin. Sometimes it got so bad that I became constipated. Because I didn't want to turn out like my father, my need to not be angry defined a great part of my life.

By suppressing my anger, it metastasized like a cancer and grew. It was only a matter of time before I became the person I desperately did not want to be. After months of pent-up anger, I would explode in anger.

Of course, the moment of anger would pass, and then I would be flooded with remorse and regret. I would apologize and try to take some responsibility for the fear I had created. But my relationships fundamentally changed as people could no longer fully trust me. Just as I had been scared of my father, those closest to me were now afraid of me.

I actively trigger the people I coach. This is a delicate subject, so I don't want to make light of it, and I want to advise that it should not be done without skill. It has taken me my whole life to learn how to do this responsibly. When we play with triggers, we can re-traumatize a person.

As I work with someone, they will give clues about a belief they hold. This belief almost always reveals itself in some sort of defense. When I find that defense, I deliberately say something I know will trigger it. The reaction comes fast, and the person will usually start giving a lot of justifications for it. However, once they are in that triggered state, I then smile and ask, "What's going on for you now?"

Sometimes the first response is "What do you mean?"

I respond in a kind and loving voice, "What happens inside of you when you hear me say that? What makes you react that way?"

Then it hits. The person will soften, and I see an awareness emerge in their eyes.

To give you an example of how this process works, here's a real-life conversation with a client, Michelle.

Michelle mentions a person she likes, and I say, "She's such a bitch." I watch her body contract. Her mouth begins moving without connecting to the feelings that come up inside of her. Before letting her continue, I ask, "What's going on?"

She stops and reflects. She says, "I felt like I needed to defend her."

"Why do you have to defend her?" I ask.

"Because she is my friend."

"I understand that. But what if you did not have to defend her? How would you interact with me differently?"

"What do you mean differently?"

"I mean, what if I said something to you, and you didn't need to defend anything. What if you didn't even know the person I was speaking about. How would you react then?"

"I guess I would be curious," she says.

"And . . ."

"I would ask you a question like, 'What makes you say that?'"

"How funny is that," I say. "If you are unattached to the person, you can be open, but once they are a friend, you have to defend them. Let's agree that defending a friend is a nice thing to do. But what I hope to help you see is how the interaction changes when you are reacting to something I've said. If you see this more broadly, you'll see how many times you do that in a day without even knowing it."

It clicks for her, and she says, "Yes, I see that I believe it's my responsibility to defend my friends. And because of that, I don't sit in connection with you. I make the defense of my friend more important than the connection we are having in this moment."

"Where does that come from?"

Tears well up in her eyes as she says, "I see a lot of sadness under all of this. I want so much to protect others that I take it on myself to do that. I take the weight of others on my shoulders because I have a very strong idea of what it means to be a good friend. Weird, I didn't even realize I was doing that until now."

She smiles and encourages me to do it again. We play the game for the next few hours. I trigger her. We stop and reflect. Each new trigger is a window to another part of herself that she is seeing with more clarity.

It may seem like a strange practice, but unless we are aware that we are reacting to a trigger, we'll mistake our beliefs as "truths." In Michelle's case, she has the belief that being a good friend means defending them when she feels they are under attack. It would be hard to argue that this is not a "good" belief to have. The challenge comes when this belief turns into a trigger.

In a triggered state, the way we interact with another changes dramatically, and that impacts how the conversation unfolds. More trigger, less connection with the other. That is why it's so important to catch our triggers. If we are aware of our triggers, we can shift how we interact and thereby stay in connection even when we feel an emotional charge.

Through the exercise, Michelle becomes more and more open. She begins to see how quickly triggers are occurring and how unaware she has been of what was happening. Until now, there has been no separation between the trigger and her response. They were one, like two sliding doors pressed so tightly against each other that they appear to be a wall unless we look closely and see the groove.

By practicing, she has the opportunity to feel the moment over and over again, until it is no longer an automatic response. There is more space to see what she is not seeing. At first she tries to solve the emotion after it has been triggered instead of seeing it the moment it occurs.

"But I don't want that feeling. How do I stop this from happening?" she says repeatedly.

I encourage her to slow down and simply observe without trying to figure it out or solve it. "We are just starting out with this. Don't try to figure it out for the moment. Experience it as a state. Allow yourself to see yourself without needing to fix anything."

What I have found is that as we see ourselves and our triggers, life gets much easier because instead of managing our emotions, we are seeing them emerge. The better able we are to see them emerge, the freer we are to play with them, and the freer we are to let them be without allowing them to define us. Rather, they guide us.

What becomes more and more apparent is that Michelle is triggered by authority, and especially by men with strong voices. I put on my strong, authoritative voice in response to something she says and say, "That's nonsense."

She's triggered. She pauses and reflects. Then, her eyes widen and she says, "Give me a moment. I am beginning to see something here. My father was incredibly loving, but he was also very strong-minded. I see that there is part of that strong-mindedness that I have never fully accepted. I have never been able to fully love."

I smile and ask, "Can you see how the inability to love and accept that part of you is also what's stopping you from loving your father?"

She nods. "Psychologically, I understand that, yet it's still hard for me to embrace that in myself. There is an aspect in it that I don't want to become."

"And what is that?"

"I don't want to lose sight that there is always another point. There is always another thing to say that is being neglected or dismissed."

"Yes, that's always true. But what happens to you when you don't have the ability to carry the weight of that voice? Not that you need to, but what happens when you can't?"

She says, "People don't necessarily know where they stand with me. By keeping things at a surface level and speaking in general terms, I ensure that people can't really get a hold of me. It's a way to protect myself. I see how this all shows up in my life. I just moved in with my husband, and we are planning to have a child together. My husband is also quite strong-minded, and I struggle to communicate important things to him because I worry that I won't be heard."

I laugh. "You married your father."

"Apparently," she laughs in return.

Her big realization comes when she says, "I see that when I get triggered, I can either step toward or away from myself. When I blindly react to a trigger, I am stepping away from myself. When I create space to explore my feelings, I am stepping toward myself."

It's as if she has a magnifying glass pointing inward at the dark spaces she's never seen before. I have seen that it is exactly in these blind triggers that we lose ourselves. To the degree that these areas go unseen, they define us and our interactions with others.

Obviously, this conversation can only happen in the context of formal coaching. I would never engage this way with someone unless they gave me explicit permission to do so. Nor do I recommend it to anyone to use in casual conversations.

Instead, my recommendation in a non-coaching scenario is to do just the opposite of the process I've just described. Rather than digging at triggers to inflame them more, a more effective approach is to use genuine curiosity, with no agenda to guide a person in any direction as a coach would.

For example, suppose you're with a friend who tells you, "You are not being authentic."

Assume for the moment that you feel triggered. You sense a need to defend. A common response in defense of yourself might be, "Well, this is who I am." Although this might not feel like a defensive response, it actually is. It is so subtle that it can be hard to catch. Instead of connecting with your friend and helping them to see and understand their projection onto you, you're creating disconnection. You're defending your belief, "I am an authentic person."

This response will likely just trigger more defensiveness in your friend. "Well, you might think so, but I don't." Or, "Of course you would say that."

The dynamic created is now tense, with the most natural of reactions—defending one's personality—becoming a moment of disconnection. In this situation, it would be easy to assume that your friend who made the original statement has created the discomfort. But that would only be partially true. Your response defines how the conversation evolves.

If you can separate yourself from the belief that you are an authentic person, then the response to the original statement could be simply, "What makes you say that?" Or, "What do you notice in my behavior that makes you say that?" Or, "It must not be easy for you if you feel that way."

In these examples, the response is not crafted to defend the hidden belief that you are an authentic person. By the same token, it is also not validating the original statement. What it does is make space for your friend to reflect on what makes them feel this way and possibly come to some new conclusions. This way of interacting is only possible when we no longer react to our own triggers unconsciously.

If I were working with you and we used this situation to explore your triggers, I would ask you what made you respond that way. This conversation might go something like this:

You: "I don't find you to be authentic."

Me: "What makes you say that?"

You: "Because when you speak, I always feel that there is something you are hiding."

Me: "Oh. That can't feel good. I don't feel like I am intentionally hiding anything, but you may be seeing something I am unaware of. What do you see specifically?"

You: "You always hesitate before you speak. Like you are looking for a way to say things diplomatically."

Me: "I don't know if it's diplomatic as much as wanting to make sure that I don't say anything that is not well considered. I'm not comfortable speaking without consideration. I see now how this may come across as being inauthentic. It's not my intention."

You: "Thank you for sharing and not pushing me away. I see that I have a certain way I like interacting, and I put that on you. I'm sorry for that."

Imagine how this approach would give you the psychological safety to explore your triggers without needing to defend or understand them. Only when we soften the grip of our triggers do we gain the power to shift our behavior.

When working with clients, I usually spend the first few weeks asking that same question over and over: "What's going on inside you right now?" It's a softer way of saying, "What's triggering you right now?" I actually prefer to not use the word "trigger" because it has the potential to be viewed as a negative thing. We can mistakenly assume that we should not have triggers. I find triggers to be a wonderful tool for cultivating self-awareness when we can turn them from a reactive to a proactive force.

In time, people begin to see the subtlety of their triggers. They begin to catch the exact moment the trigger occurs and navigate the moments with more grace and agility.

I like to look at triggers through the lens of aikido. Aikido is a form of martial arts from Japan where practitioners are taught to use the force and momentum of their opponents as the source of power. We can either react to the force of triggers with more force or instead use the momentum of the energy coming toward us to create more self-awareness.

✳ ✳ ✳

Lesson: Triggers point us in the direction of healing.

Exercise 5: Trigger Me Blind

Looking at our own triggers can be challenging because once we turn defensive, it's almost impossible for us to see ourselves in this defensive state. It usually comes afterward, when we have come down from the triggered state and feel a sense of unease. In the following exercise, Trigger Me Blind, we will dig into your triggers to better understand what's behind them.

What triggers you most?

Parents (e.g., commenting on your life or judging choices you have made)

A partner (e.g., discussions around money, work, sex)

A sibling (e.g., dealing with expectations and assumptions)

People at work (e.g., treating you disrespectfully or without consideration)

People talking in movie theaters

People showing up late

Traffic jams

Money

Dishonesty

Death

Public speaking

Other: _____

_____

_____

Take the triggers you have chosen and answer two questions about them:

1 How do I react to these when I am triggered today?

2 What would an alternative look like if I were to be less charged?

Normal response when triggered:

"That's not true."

"What are you talking about?"

"I am sick of you saying that!"

"I am annoyed."

"Bullshit."

Other: _____

_____

_____

A less triggered alternative:

"How did you come to that conclusion?"

"What makes you say that?"

"That's hard for me to hear."

"That's not easy for me."

"What are you feeling now?"

"That sounds like a challenge."

Other: _____
_____
_____

In reflecting on your answers, you may see that there are things that you do reactively because they trigger a deep emotion. It can be hard to look at that emotion and not want to defend it. It often comes from a deep wound or a strong belief. In making space to feel where the trigger is coming from, we create space inside of ourselves for healing—not only in ourselves but also in our relationships with others. In becoming less reactive, we are able to interact with more love and compassion, which shifts our relationships from defensive to connected.

CHAPTER 6

Expectations Don't Listen

A coaching client calls and asks, "Andy, I'm in trouble. My parents are angry that we decided not to visit them for the holidays."

"What did they say?" I ask.

"They just kept repeating, 'Holidays are family time.' I tried to explain that we really wanted to see them, but it was a tough year and we needed to get away. That only got them angrier. My mom told me, 'We have been planning for this all year long, and you don't consider us.' That call happened two weeks ago, and we have not spoken since. Clearly, they have the idea that we will be with them every year, but that's unreasonable to expect."

We can't discuss triggers without also discussing expectations. They are another of life's great paradoxes. We need them, yet they are ticking time bombs in relationships.

Expectations are neither good nor bad; they simply are a requirement of living because they are the only way to manage the complexity of life. Imagine telling a highly organized partner, "We're leaving on a train tomorrow," and not give them a time. Or trying to get a complex project done without deciding the roles. It simply does not work. Failing to understand and establish expectations is a recipe for disaster.

Here's where it gets exciting. Some of our expectations are more conscious to us than others. We will call the expectations we're less conscious of "blind expectations." These are tricky because they are a byproduct of our beliefs. And as mentioned earlier, when a belief starts to define us and our thoughts, we are easily triggered and incapable of self-reflection. When we meet a person with differing beliefs, the conversation can quickly turn into an argument.

Expectations are so challenging because they have an implicit goal or outcome associated with them. Until we get there, we are in tension. This future state becomes the focus of our efforts, and we become agitated when we don't succeed. This is how the future rules us in the present.

Her: "We've been dating for two years, and it's time for us to get married. It's what people do."

Him: "I'm just not ready yet. Everything is great. Why the hurry?"

Her: "What do you mean hurry? We have been dating two years. Are you serious about us?"

Him: "Of course."

Her: "Then why are you stringing me along?"

We hear in the above interaction an expectation from the woman that two years is enough time to decide to get married. The goal is marriage. That goal perhaps comes from a mix of socialization, social pressure, and a touch of Disney movies. With that goal in mind, she now blames her partner for not agreeing to her expectation. What she does not see is that she is holding a belief, which is of course her prerogative, but she cannot then blame another for holding a different belief.

Here is how this interaction might look like without the belief:

Her: "Honey, I've been thinking about us and wondering what your thoughts were on marriage."

Him: "I haven't really thought about it. I feel like we are still young and we have time to make that decision."

Her: "I understand that you are not jumping at the opportunity.

I would love it if we could talk about it because it is important to me, and I do want to know your feelings on it."

In this exchange, we see that the woman has not denied her desire to get married, but at the same time, she has not allowed her expectation to define the way she interacts around the subject. She creates space for a discussion, which may or may not lead to her desired outcome. The critical point is that she does not impose an expectation upon her partner and then blame him for it—a common recipe for disaster in relationships.

While expectations help us focus and get things done, they simultaneously create tension and prevent people from seeing one another. We are so eager to get to the outcome that we ignore the consequences. When someone fails to meet our expectations, how easy would it be for us to ask them, "How are you doing?" and truly mean it? When people violate our expectations, we often judge them without even being aware that we're doing that. We see this reflected in words like "should" or "inappropriate."

Take the word "should." "He should have told us he was going to be late." "We should have had a child by now." "Shouldn't he be out of the house already?" In all these examples, the person speaking is looking at the situation with an expectation.

In the first example of the friend who is late, the expectation is time. If a time is agreed upon, it "should" be honored. The belief behind this expectation is probably something like, "It's disrespectful to leave someone waiting." Or, "You are not valuing other people's time." Again, this is not to say that we are not allowed to have these expectations. It's only to clarify that a belief is what makes a person feel slighted or disrespected.

In the second example of having a child by a certain age, typically a larger societal belief has existed for multiple generations and implicitly pushes people to get married or have children by a certain age. It's common for people to use this societal expectation as an excuse to blame or shame another, especially someone who does not proceed according to the desired timetable.

The relationship challenges that arise from expectations grow exponentially when expectations are broadened to a societal level. Religion, schooling, and culture combine to create a powerful belief system that has its own embedded expectations—things like by what age we should be married, when we should have kids, and even when we eat dinner and how often we take showers.

I have a friend, Mary, who decided not to have children. When she told her parents, she was chastised, "Why are you so selfish? You don't think of anyone but yourself." Here we see that Mary made a choice that was at odds with the expectations of her parents. Instead of her parents processing that disappointment, they turned to blame. This is a challenge faced by many as they navigate the societal expectations of others.

With this backdrop of social pressure, we are constantly adapting to accommodate so that we can belong, or at least not offend others. Consider the innocence of typical questions like, "When are we going to have grandchildren?" Or, "We've been going out for three years. Isn't it time we got married?" Our beliefs quickly translate into expectations of how things should be.

Think for a moment. What things have you been holding on to as expectations without ever knowing? They are not easy to pinpoint.

The answer to this is certainly not to stop having expectations. That would be absurd. The answer is to heighten our awareness around these expectations so that we can navigate them with grace. A quote from Carl Jung comes to mind: "Until you make the unconscious conscious, it will direct your life and you will call it fate."

When embraced wisely, expectations can be powerful tools in communication. Unfortunately, this is rarely the case. More often than not, expectations are unseen. And unseen, unspoken expectations turn into resentment when they are unmet. This then triggers defensiveness in those of whom we have expectations.

So how do we shift this? How do we make it so that you can be you and I can be me, without our unconscious expectations separating us? The answer to this is both simple and incredibly difficult: it's to realize that *my* expectations are not *your* problem. I get to have my expectations. But I do not get to blame you for them. Instead of harboring resentment, I can share my expectations, and we can discuss and reflect together. In short, we can connect by owning and sharing our expectations rather than allowing expectation to separate us from others.

I was once working with a couple where the husband had a lot of expectations around money, and particularly how it should be spent. "She buys frivolous things," he said. "Although we can afford it, she's not respecting the money I earn."

She retorted, "I appreciate the money you make. And I don't think it's asking too much to do something to take care of myself once a week."

"It's not just once a week," he argued. "You get coffee every day. If you do the math, that costs us $1,000 a year."

I could continue with this story, but you already know where it's heading. Each spouse has a clear expectation of how to spend money, but neither is sharing where that expectation has come from. What is causing this argument? The fact that they are using their subjective expectations as "facts." He thinks she should be spending less money. She thinks he should see why her self-care is so important.

When we make our expectations conscious and translate them into observations and understandings of ourselves, then we can bring them forward in a way that is less likely to trigger another. For example, the above conversation could change to the husband saying something like, "I see that you have been buying coffees every day [observation]. I must admit that makes me nervous [observation of SELF]. I've been looking at the bank account, and I'm scared that we may run out of money soon."

This approach removes the superior position ("I'm right and

you're wrong; let me explain why") from the conversation. From an equal position, he is talking about the impact of her behavior on both of them. Although he still has expectations, he is owning them and not imposing them on her. This removes his blame toward her, which then makes it much less likely that she will respond defensively.

As I said, expectations are neither good nor bad. They are thoughts and beliefs we are either conscious of or not. Blind expectations become judgment disguised as righteousness: "I know something you don't. You are less than me if you don't comply with my norms or societal norms."

When I was living in Japan, I was unaware of the social norms. I once took a tissue and blew my nose in public, only to be taken aside and told in the politest of ways, "That is considered impolite here." What I learned in that moment was something quite transformational. A society had defined what was and was not polite. In many ways, it was arbitrary. Who gets to decide that blowing your nose in public is an offense? And yet it had become a society norm, normalized and imposed onto others with judgment if not followed. This judgment is typically accompanied by shame in order to force people into compliance.

Imposing our expectations on others—especially when we aren't aware that we're doing it—is one of the most surefire ways to disconnect from a person. No one likes to feel judged or to feel that they are disappointing people by not living up to expectations. When we blindly impose our expectations onto another, we subconsciously—yet clearly—send the message that this person isn't good enough. By owning our expectations, we can communicate them without alienating others in the process.

✳ ✳ ✳

Lesson: Blind expectations wreak havoc in relationships.

Exercise 6: Check It Out

Sometimes it's hard to see that we are bringing our expectations into a relationship. In the Check It Out exercise, you are asked to distinguish between an observation and an expectation. For each of the situations listed below, check the box where it belongs.

Statement	Observation	Expectation
It is normal to get married after dating.	○	○
There are 365 days in a year.	○	○
Kids should be out of the house by twenty-one years old.	○	○
She will leave the house at twenty-one years old.	○	○
It's important to get good grades in school.	○	○
One-night stands are wrong.	○	○
Music soothes the soul.	○	○
I listen to soul music.	○	○
People should be able to speak a second language.	○	○
It will be seventy degrees tomorrow.	○	○
It is seventy degrees now.	○	○
A family house should have a garden.	○	○
We are going to Spain next month.	○	○
When the floor is dirty, mice will come.	○	○
I sing in front of crowds.	○	○
The medicine will cure the cold.	○	○
Twenty percent of the population speaks Spanish.	○	○
He was five minutes late to the meeting.	○	○
Meetings should start on time.	○	○

You may have noticed that it is not always easy to distinguish an observation from an expectation. In some cases, expectations are so much a part of who we are that they can be hard to recognize. Or even harder to let go of. Don't worry: that is not being asked of you. Sensing these expectations, and when they turn into triggers, will take some practice. Knowing that they exist and beginning to make space to respond differently is a start.

CHAPTER 7

Assume at Your Own Risk

Assumptions are very similar to their counterpart, expectations. However, they have a unique quality that is important to note. Where expectation often comes from the projection of an outcome in the future, an assumption often comes from an interpretation of what someone has done or said. The most obvious examples occur around word usage. Although everyone applies different meaning to words, we have a hidden belief that the meaning we have given a word is somehow universal—as if we have been ordained with a monopoly on proper language usage.

I learned this lesson often in Japan. I remember many challenges regarding the word "no." In the United States, it is commonly heard. One asks a question, and they are given a simple yes or no answer. In Japan, it is impolite to say no directly. Instead, there is often a bending of the head and a long, drawn-out sigh with words attached: "Sou ka na," roughly translated as, "Really."

It took me half a year to finally understand that I was in fact being told no, although the word itself was never stated. My assumption was that we all have a word for no and that we all use it similarly. Although this is quite an extreme example, the same assumptions are made daily in ways that we are often unaware of.

The same paradox that exists for expectations also exists for assumptions. We need to make assumptions when interacting. But in doing so, we constantly risk creating triggers by potentially making false interpretations. The challenge with assumptions is that we often don't even recognize when we're making them. Our interpretations happen so quickly and are taken so seriously that we turn them into "facts" and blame another.

> Him: "I told you that it would be done, and I did it."
> Her: "What do you mean, 'done'? It's not even close to being done."
> Him: "I don't know what you are talking about. Have you looked? It's done."
> Her: "No, it's not."

The whole idea is actually quite insane. We hear someone use certain words to which he has applied meaning. His meaning is different than the meaning that his partner has applied, yet each accepts his or her own interpretation.

When I listen to couples arguing, the contention almost always revolves around an assumption that one is making about the other, often concerning the meaning of words. Instead of either partner giving space to create a common understanding of what the other means, an assumption is made by each that their definition is the "right" one.

These are very typical interactions that occur in homes every day. Each person has a different interpretation of what "done" means. Furthermore, we can easily see how these interpretations turn into judgment and blame of the other. The husband feels exasperated and may view the wife as "nagging." The wife judges the husband for being "lazy" and "irresponsible."

When I hear such arguments, a voice in my head always yells, "ASK!" If we took a moment to ask questions, things would look dramatically different. Sadly, when we don't ask what people mean by the words they use, we fall back to using our assumptions as further justification to judge and point fingers.

> Her: "You said that you would help."
> Him: "I did."
> Her: "Helping is not dropping by a few times and saying hello."

Him: "I asked if I could do anything, and she said she was okay."

Her: "Help is when you get groceries and clean things up in the house!"

Think of that for a moment. We make an interpretation that ignores another's and then use that as a justification to blame him or her. This happens constantly, and people have no idea what's even happening.

With more consciousness, here's how a situation could be handled differently:

Her: "Honey, I just looked in the garden, and I see that the things I expected to be done are not. When you told me it was done, what did you mean?"

Him: "You asked me to clean up the leaves, right?"

Her: "That was only part of it. I was hoping that you would also cut back the hedges and mow the grass."

Him: "Oh, I was planning on doing that next week because it's closer to the party."

In this example, both of them have an interpretation of what "done" means. But since they are making those interpretations clear, they can get on the same page without judgments, blame, and conflict.

This scenario could become even more conscious and productive if different questions are asked.

Her: "Honey, I'd like to have the garden cleaned up next week so we can get ready for the party."

Him: "Sure."

Her: "What do you think would be good to do for the party?"

Him: "I am planning on doing the leaves this weekend and the rest a few days before so it looks nice."

Her: "I'm a bit anxious that you won't have time if you wait. You know how busy you get. Could you do it all this weekend?"

In this interaction, we see that less is being taken for granted. One might argue that the wife is managing the husband, but in actuality she is taking responsibility for her expectations. She is not taking anything for granted, which would then turn into assumptions.

I've spent a lot of my coaching time supporting people to communicate in a way that allows fewer and fewer assumptions to be made regarding their words. This is done though a term that has been overused throughout the years, but I use it nonetheless: vulnerability.

When we show ourselves in an interaction, the likelihood that another will misinterpret us decreases considerably. It's easier for people to see our intentions and not just hear our words.

Going back to our example, here are three different ways the wife could ask her husband for assistance:

Method #1: "Please do the garden this weekend."

Method #2: "I'm anxious that we may not have enough time if we don't do it this weekend."

Method #3: "I know you have other things to do, but if you can make time for this, I'd really appreciate it. I've got a lot on my mind, and this has been weighing on me."

You see through these examples that she shows more and more of herself. And in the last, she also shows appreciation for what she is asking. When I'm interacting with others, I like to show as much of myself as possible so as not to be misinterpreted or leave room for assumptions. This may take a little more time, but I've always found that it saves a lot of time, energy, hassle, and aggravation later.

✳ ✳ ✳

Lesson: Assumptions are best wrapped in questions.

Exercise 7: Assume Away

As pointed out, some of the biggest assumptions that we make are around the words or phrases others use. In the following exercise, there is a list of sentences, each with a word that would be easy to make assumptions about. Pick the word in each sentence that has the highest likelihood to be misinterpreted and form a question. I'll give the first examples to start:

I want it done well.

"What do you mean when you say 'well'?"
"How does 'well' look to you?"
"What would you expect to see if it was done 'well'?"

How about we arrange to get it done next week?

"When you say 'done,' what are you expecting?"
"What day next week were you thinking?"

You are trying too hard.

"What do you mean by 'too'?"

_____

_____

I'm getting frustrated with you.

"Frustrated how?"

_____

_____

The class needs to change.

"What do you think needs to change?"

_____

_____

The house is dirty.

"How is it dirty?"

_____

_____

As you look at your answers, contemplate where conversations in your past may have gone awry. How might it have been different if you had applied this approach? Are you willing to let go of some of your assumptions and ask questions to improve your interactions? Although it can feel like a big time waster, in the end it will save a lot of stress.

LISTEN TO THE CHAPTER

CHAPTER 8

Giving Our Power Away with Codependency

We often see things in people that we judge and even want to change about them. We need them to be someone other than who they are in order for us to feel safe and comfortable. The term used for one state that results from this dynamic is "codependence."

Codependence has two sides, hence the prefix "co." The form of codependence I'd like to focus on is the one I see most often, where one partner gives away his or her power in a relationship.

Oftentimes, one partner will have a stronger nature than the other. They will state their opinion more firmly or make stronger judgments. When a relationship is starting out, this can work well, as the two will complement one another, one more dominant and the other more submissive. What I've often seen is that over time, unknowingly, while the stronger of the two believes that they are helping, they are actually taking away the other's self-confidence.

This shows up in different ways. A slight comment: "I know how things are done, and this certainly will not work." Or, "You're going to fail if you do it that way." Or it may be far more pointed: "That's not for you," or, "Leave that for the qualified people."

This is not usually done with intention or malice, yet there are consequences. A very confident person can inadvertently make others feel insecure, which in turn causes them to lose confidence—or the phrase I often use is "give away their agency." In the dominant person's enthusiasm, they fail to consider the ability of their partner to take in the message without sabotaging their confidence.

This pattern has very much been a part of my life. A common thread has run through all of my relationships, and I see it in many of my clients today. I like to call it the "fixer" archetype. It can be summarized in the following sentence: "I love you, and I can help you be a stronger and more confident person."

For me, the process looked like this: I would meet a woman, most often soft-spoken, and feel an attraction and a deep desire to protect her. In many ways, I was attracted to her because of this need to protect. On a subtle level, I was aware of her insecurities, and I felt that I could help her overcome them.

Instead of loving her for who she was, I would first begin to suggest, then recommend, and finally direct. The progression went along these lines: "Have you thought about doing a course?" This increased to, "I think it would be great if you did a course." And finally, in desperation, "You've got to do a course. It's time."

When that no longer worked, my frustration grew. I'd begin to blame my partner for not doing what I believed was right. This would turn into arguments, which eventually led to an emotional shutdown in myself and eventually with her. I needed my partner to be something that she was not so that I could make peace inside of myself.

Early in my relationship with Rani, I was just learning about self-development and was utterly convinced of my own understanding. I spent a great deal of my time telling her what she did not understand. I remember arguing with her as she shared challenges she faced at work while refusing to attend any of my trainings. In my mind, these courses would solve all of her problems.

Thankfully, she resisted. But in trying to convince her that she did not know something, I was blindly trying to create a hole in her psyche that I could fill with my understanding. Obviously, this was quite arrogant.

When we communicate with others, either we can give them

more clarity in their own understanding and help them gain more confidence, or we can make them less confident. It would be incorrect to say that one is good or bad. Sometimes people can use a bit of straight talk, and other times they benefit from a loving embrace. Yet if we are not aware of our ability to undermine another's confidence, then we are very likely to inadvertently take it away, in order to fulfill our need to fix them.

I once supported a couple struggling with this dynamic. For years, the wife had not stood up for herself, and when she finally did, the conversation went something like this:

Wife: "You are always critical of me. You always tell me what I'm doing wrong."

Husband: "Honey, it's not that you are doing it wrong. I'm only trying to point out what's going on."

Wife: "You always say that. You act like you know better than me and that your view is better than mine."

Husband: "No, honey, I'm just trying to share how I see things so that you understand where I'm coming from in all of this."

Wife: "No, you're not. You're trying to convince me, like you always do."

What we see here is what happens when a person who has given away their agency for a time begins to take it back. Instead of leading to a beautiful celebration, it often turns into a fight. The wife blames the husband for taking it from her, never quite realizing that she gave it away. With all the pent-up frustration, she now pushes her partner away. It's hard for people to celebrate this moment because it's often filled with resentment.

This chapter may feel as if it is pointing at the same problem over and over again in different ways, and it is. I spend time here so that we can begin to understand how to avoid losing ourselves in our relationship with others.

I wish that I could give you an easy formula, but this process is actually a journey that each partner takes individually. When we enter a partnership, we meet a person at one moment in our and their lives. With some luck, we will evolve to become very different people over the course of our relationship. The capacity that allows a couple to navigate these changes is the ability to listen closely to ourselves and trust in what we are hearing.

There is a trap we fall into when we stop listening to ourselves. Once we no longer use our own experience as the measurement, we lose agency over our own thinking and our learning process. It's in these moments that we hand our power over to another. We tell ourselves that we don't know something as well as another and that we "need them."

This creates a unique challenge in relationships. We are hopefully in relationships so that our partners can support us, even push us forward at times. Where is the boundary between support and codependence?

At times, we cannot deny that our partners are exhibiting behaviors that don't serve them. But who are we to change them? Who is to say that the change we want for others is relevant or important for them? What if they need to fail in order to learn an important lesson?

The distinction that helps address this challenge is a question we need to ask ourselves: "How can I support my partner in his or her developmental process? If I assume that I cannot teach them and instead support them in their own process, how can I do that best?" This is a far leap from telling our partner what they do not understand, and it forces us to question ourselves, not them.

This is an important nuance when it comes to supporting others. I've seen so many people who are so self-absorbed that they fail to see the harm they cause in their partners. Not surprisingly, the partner who is trying to "teach" often blames the other for not understanding, thereby reinforcing the insecurity.

In a loving relationship, we must balance our own perceived understanding of what is better for the other with their development on their timetable. If we are motivated by our own frustration to try to change another, we are trying to expand that person's *understanding* but not necessarily increasing their *awareness*. By "understanding," I'm referring to intellectual knowledge of why things are the way they are. Trying to make others "understand" simply means imposing our own perspective on them. Trying to help others raise their awareness is about helping them find their own answers.

Our desire to share what we know is strong. It gives us a sense of control. When we know something, we feel confident. We feel less vulnerable. And therein lies the trap. That is where we start imposing our knowledge on others.

Personally, I'm far less concerned with what I believe I know and more concerned with helping others develop, in whatever way I can. I do not choose the time frame for this. It may be a day. It may be a year. It may be a lifetime. Cultivating healthy relationships requires presence—being present to our own needs and wants while also making space for the needs and wants of others.

How a conversation shifts from one paradigm to another looks something like this:

"I hate my job."

As this has been repeated for years, the urge may be to say, with a sense of agitation, "You've been discussing this for years now. Why don't you do something about it?"

If we flip this to the intention of supporting, one might say with a loving concern, "You've been discussing this for years now. How does it feel to be dealing with this for so long?"

In the first response, I need something from my partner emotionally. I need them to do something about it. The agitation bleeds into the discussion, and instead of feeling safe to explore, they are certain to shut down. In the latter example, I am simply supporting them on their journey. I am not trying to get them anywhere but rather helping them feel into their own emotional state, which may or may not help them see themselves more clearly. Most importantly, I am not dependent on them doing anything about it.

As much as we may want to, we cannot manage another person's experience. We also cannot stop a person from giving away his or her agency. What can only heighten our awareness of when this occurs. We can see the instances when we feel less than another. We can watch our thinking as we go from confident to insecure in an instant.

On a coaching call, a client shared with me that she had a job interview and it went poorly. She said, "The CEO was a strong woman, and I saw that I was not comfortable when she asked me questions."

"Where do you see this coming from?" I asked.

She responded, "Well, I saw her picture online before the interview, and I already felt a bit insecure going in."

"That's interesting," I said. "What from your past might make that understandable?"

She said, "I was the second child in my family, and my sister was the oldest. When we were young, my parents would often call me by her name. I never felt like I had my own identity."

"And how was that for you?" I asked.

"Well, I was shy and didn't like to talk. I would remain silent most of the time. I was often judged for this, and I even remember getting a failing grade on my report card for not speaking up in class."

"And how did that affect you?"

"It only made me turn more inward. I had a lot of judgment toward strong and confident people. People who said what they felt. People who took up space."

"You judged them," I said. "It sounds like you still do."

"What do you mean?" she asked.

I answered, "Well, when you saw the image of the CEO, what did you associate with her?"

"Strength and confidence," she replied.

"Okay," I said. "And if you were strong and confident, would you be intimidated by her?"

"No."

"What stops you from being strong and confident? And when you answer, think about what we've already talked about."

"I see that I turn back into the shy little girl. I don't allow myself to be strong because I don't think it's good."

"And why is that not good?" I pressed.

"Because you should think about others. It's not all about you."

"So when people are strong, it's all about them?"

"I see that I feel that way. I judge people who are strong, and I see that it makes me feel weak."

She's a client I've worked with for years, so she is very familiar with the radical self-acceptance exercise I detail in my previous book, *The Wounded Healer*. The exercise is to simply state out loud the beliefs we have the hardest time accepting and then say, "And it's okay."

I suggested, "How about if you said, 'I'm weak and incapable, and it's okay.' 'I judge strong people, and it's okay.' 'I'm never going to be as strong as my sister, and it's okay.'"

She repeated the statements one after another, and laughter and tears emerged. She said, "I see that I give my agency away to strong people because I never learned to be strong myself. Instead of celebrating their strength and welcoming it into my own life, I judge it in them and get further and further away from it myself."

"Yes, that's it," I acknowledged. "Love your perceived weakness, and it will soon become your greatest strength."

Being codependent on others means we give our power to them. We are dependent on how they behave in order for us to be okay. To lose codependence, we must take back our agency and power. This comes as we stop blaming others and take responsibility for how we have given away our own agency.

Lesson: Trust yourself enough to let others be themselves.

Exercise 8: Stop the Madness

As this chapter has detailed, codependent relationships can make you crazy. In this exercise, you will be presented with several situations, and you get to choose how to react. Some answers will lean more in the direction of codependent relationships; others will not.

It's your friend's/partner's birthday, and you spent weeks thinking up the perfect gift. You give it to them, but they don't react as you would have liked.

- (A) You feel a sense of frustration but don't mention it because it is their birthday.
- (B) You tell them that you expected them to be happier.
- (C) You bottle it all up and feel disappointed.
- (D) You get frustrated with them for not appreciating your efforts.
- (E) None of the above.

Your partner/friend has been struggling in the office for weeks. You see them getting so worked up that you are worried they are going to get health issues.

- (A) You tell them that they need to stop working.
- (B) You remain quiet and do your best to make sure everything is organized for them.
- (C) You take care of them as well as you can until the moment passes.
- (D) You get frustrated with them because they certainly know better.
- (E) None of the above.

Your partner/friend is always in an argument with one of their siblings. Recently, they have begun to behave in very adolescent ways.

Ⓐ You tell them to grow up.

Ⓑ You arrange a meeting for the two to talk.

Ⓒ You joke about it so you can cope.

Ⓓ You tell them how you dealt with your siblings.

Ⓔ None of the above.

Your partner/friend is working so hard that you are feeling neglected.

Ⓐ You blame them for the way you are feeling.

Ⓑ You present an ultimatum: "Your phone or me."

Ⓒ You wait around until they have time for you.

Ⓓ You make snide remarks each time they pick up the phone.

Ⓔ None of the above.

RECAP

Being in a codependent relationship can be tough. We can simultaneously love and hate someone, so much so that we never really know how to separate the two feelings. In all the above questions, the "correct" answer is "e) None of the above." Having said that, there are times when I would say "a" through "d," so it is very much connected to the context and the intention. The intention of this exercise was to highlight the moments that we take care of the other and neglect ourselves. There is of course a balance when we are in relationships. The most important point is to be conscious of that balance and manage it when it starts to shift.

CHAPTER RECAP VIDEO

CHAPTER 9

I'm Right, You're Wrong

For many years, I have had a hard time watching news television. The programming is primarily focused on ratcheting up differences of opinion to attract viewership. Like driving past an accident, it's hard to avert your eyes. The unfortunate byproduct of this is that people get further and further caught up in the idea of right and wrong. A show which exemplified this was *Crossfire*. The two hosts would take differing stances on a subject and crank up the intensity by bringing on guests who would polarize the situation even further.

An episode where they invited the comedian Jon Stewart left a deep impression on me. Stewart did his best to point out the damage of deep-rooted beliefs.

"When you have people on for just reactionary, knee-jerk—" Stewart said, before the host interrupted him with, "I thought you were going to be funny."

Stewart finished, "You have a responsibility to the public discourse, and you fail miserably."

What he was pointing out, with no reception from either host, was how the format of right and wrong is polarizing. After taking one side and making no effort to understand an opposing argument, we divide. We divide so deeply that it's hard, if not impossible, to see another person. To understand the consequences of this, we need look no further than the state of political discourse today.

One of the biggest unseen obstacles in relationships is the

belief that we possess the "truth." This unexamined belief creates the dynamic, "I'm right and you're wrong," which is obviously disconnecting and can be devastating in relationships. This self-righteous truth is now very much a part of everyday life.

Of course, people do their best to disguise this by saying things like, "It's my truth" or, "This is how I experienced it." However, there are two problems with this line of thinking. Firstly, it shows no vulnerability. Secondly, it presumes that our way of seeing things is not already flawed.

If we take the opposite extreme and convince ourselves that we know nothing, that would create a lot of openness but deny the understanding and insight of our life experiences. This all leads us to an important paradox in relationships: "How can I be simultaneously *certain* and *open*?" That is the space where our consciousness evolves quickly because we are receptive to new input, without defense. This state is both receptive and expansive.

When we take what we know as a working assumption and live from it while remaining completely open, life becomes a grand experiment. We grow swiftly because we are making conscious assumptions and learning from the feedback. We are not looking to confirm our reality—going back to the term "confirmation bias." Instead, we navigate life as if it's an incomplete map to which we add details as we travel further and further. As I stated earlier, assumptions are not a bad thing, but they are detrimental if we don't know we're making them and they slowly creep into becoming our truth.

I don't want to pretend like holding your truths lightly is easy. I have had to fight through many demons to give up some of my "truths," and they still come up on occasion. To dig into this further, let's take a look at a topic that can create deep division:

"The vaccine is dangerous. The doctor who invented the technology even advises against it."

"But the studies have proven that it's safe and effective."

"Oh, I see you are buying the mainstream media narrative. When are you going to start thinking for yourself? You're being fed a bunch of lies, and you're believing it."

"Actually, I have done a lot of research, and I don't believe these are lies. You are the one being fed the lies. I am making an informed decision."

I use this specific example because it is a hot topic and it is important not to shy away from things that are difficult to discuss. We could take either side of this subject and create a truth. I can already hear both arguments. The feeling is, "You must take a side. People are dying." Interestingly enough, both sides are making the same argument.

This book is not trying to convince you of one side or the other. What it is trying to point out is that once we treat our side as "truth," there is no space for a dialogue. If there is no dialogue, then we are not meeting another person in the middle; rather, we are asking them to come to our side or go away. Imagine two people holding different truths coming together. What are the chances that either will listen to the other?

To shift this confining way of interacting, let's play a thought experiment. Think of someone with whom you are very close and you know very well. Someone whose behavior is highly predictable. Instead of thinking you know that person, imagine that you know nothing about them. Witness how your brain begins to shift. See how curiosity begins to emerge. In this process of undoing what you "know," you sense a new space emerge. It's in that space of not knowing where deep creativity emerges. And this way of being has very direct consequences.

It's only possible to function in this state if we are not attached to the idea of truth. Following that logic, it's often great to test our working assumption. For instance, if we think that our partner is always late because she does not leave time between her last meeting and her next, we might ask, "By the way, how much time do you leave between meetings?" She may say, "None." Or she may say, "Ten minutes." Now, instead of our assumption becoming a disconnecting judgment, our genuine curiosity can allow for greater connection.

The understanding that allowed me the freedom to let go of truth and still be certain was this statement from Aristotle: "The more you know, the more you know that you don't know." Every time I thought I knew something, I saw that I was creating that reality through confirmation bias—only seeing the things that confirmed what I thought I knew. I can be certain that I am uncertain. That may sound dumb, but it is the foundation of great confidence.

My mentor, Cees de Bruin, helped me discover this understanding when he recommended that I read a book by the philosopher Karl Popper, *Conjectures and Refutations*. In a nutshell, Popper said there is no absolute truth. Nothing can be said as fact. This was at odds with everything I had learned in college. The scientific method was created for that very purpose—so we could make hypotheses and test them, and in that testing, come to objective conclusions. But according to Popper, all we can ever do is make a statement and define the context in which the statement is true. For example, the statement, "Water boils at 100 degrees Celsius." In scientific terms, this would be true. But Popper would point out that the statement can only be true if conditions are added. For example, "Water boils at 100 degrees Celsius *if* the water has no sodium content and it is boiled at sea level." Otherwise, the statement is not true.

This understanding turned my thinking upside down. Before reading the book, I was living in the land of right and wrong, the land of "he said, she said." Afterward, I was sitting with a new reality: *Everyone is right all the time.* Just as Popper said, people define the context for the statement they are making. Knowing this, how can I disagree with anything?

This enables one to live in a defenseless state. If someone calls me an idiot, they are in fact correct. What I do not know is the context they have for saying that. Of course, this does not mean that I am *only* an idiot. It just means they likely have a context in which that statement is true.

In this awareness, I became full of questions. I was no longer interested in proving my point correct. Rather, I grew curious about what context the other was considering when making his or her statement. If I ever found myself conflicted, it would be resolved in the discovery of the context. If someone said something I didn't understand or disagreed with, or if I felt myself reacting, I would just sit in wonder about the context they must be referring to. In what context was what they were saying true? The only way I could figure out the context was by asking genuinely curious questions.

I stopped defending or trying to convince people of my position. Instead, I would simply ask, "What makes you say that?" Thus, I found myself learning from each discussion. Instead of getting more set in my ways, I learned to flow freely. I learned to listen closely and create meaningful relationships I never thought possible.

Once we understand that everyone creates their own truth through the context they create, our life changes. Imagine what happens when we are free to see that we have ideas about how things are and, at the same time, others have their own ideas. When we do not have the burden of holding on to truth, we can simply ask questions to understand the context of the other. If we are not asking questions, rest assured that we are either defending or trying to make a point. This is not a problem, but it is worth noting, as there are easy ways to recognize that we are stuck in the idea that we have the truth.

If we go back to the discussion around the vaccines, the discussion would look very different if one or both of the people did not come from a place of "truth."

"The vaccine is dangerous. The doctor who invented the technology even advises against it."

"I see that this is very important for you. What if I told you that I know it is a risk but it's one that I am willing to take?"

"Yes, but you do not know the risk that you are taking."

"I guess I don't, but it is a choice that I am making based on the research that I have done."

"But you are only looking at the resources that have been manipulated by the media."

"That may be so, but they are the resources that I have decided to look at, and I know that they have their own potential biases. It is a personal decision, and each person needs to make it for themselves. I may be wrong, but it's my decision, with all its possible consequences."

In this interaction, we see a shift to openness and ease. When we hold opinions lightly, a whole new world of freedom opens up to us. In the world of "truth," we need to be right, and we very much need others to know our opinions. However, if our intention in a relationship is connection, then we don't need the other person to understand our views. They are either interested and they ask, or they are not interested.

Trying to get others interested in our opinions is exhausting and often leads to frustration on both sides. For example, my wife, Rani, has never found my work interesting. In fact, she hasn't even read any of my books. We both appreciate that she leads her life and I lead my own. If I needed her to become a fan of my work, I would feel judgment and resentment toward her. Instead, I love her for having her own interests and supporting me, even if my work is not of interest to her.

When we let go of needing to know the truth and needing to be right, life gets easier. We have nothing to defend, so we can be much more open. Our whole system calms down. We ask better questions. And ultimately, we find it much easier to connect with others.

✳ ✳ ✳

Lesson: If you need to be "right," you're going the wrong way.

Exercise 9: Truth or Dare

Following the work of Karl Popper, there are a number of statements below. Knowing that each person creates their own reality with a context that they decide on, what are questions you could ask to figure out the other's context for making the statement?

"What makes you say that?"
"What have I done?"
"Where do you see that?"

This is a stupid idea.

"How do you see it as stupid?"

_____

_____

What's your problem?

"What do you mean?"

_____

_____

How could you say that?

_____
_____
_____

You are not that smart.

_____
_____
_____

Mainstream media is so biased.

_____
_____
_____

Aliens do exist.

_____
_____
_____

It is not always easy to see where our truth gets in the way of creating meaningful relationships. For many, holding the truth is more important than connecting with others. This must not be judged negatively. We all get to decide what we want to fight for and where we want to create more space for connection. This chapter hopes to heighten the awareness that we always have a choice.

SECTION III

Opening the Door to Connection

LISTEN TO THE
CHAPTER

CHAPTER 10

Personal Responsibility Is the Start

I was thirty years old. I had a few failed relationships behind me and a lifetime of repressed emotions inside me that were bleeding into all aspects of my life. I remember the moment well. I looked into the mirror and said, "The only thing consistent in all your failed relationships is you."

In that moment, I no longer fully trusted myself. Another one of life's great paradoxes: in order to become trustworthy, we must first be able to acknowledge that we cannot fully trust ourselves.

In this admission, I found humility. I shifted my communication to be more of an intuitive dance rather than a forced march driven by logical principles. I spent less time telling people what I thought and more time asking questions. Everything I've shared so far in this book was only made possible because in that moment, I no longer accepted that I knew what I was doing. I decided to listen to myself and others more attentively.

When I look back on my life, I see that my opportunities have come from my ability to communicate—my ability to make people feel seen and heard. At sixteen years old, I started selling suits to people three or four times my age. In my twenties, I was hired as a marketing director for a company that was weeks away from going public—and I had no marketing experience whatsoever. I simply had communication skills.

However, those skills were largely intuitive and unconscious. Although I was skilled, I also had many blind spots, which created problems in my relationships. It wasn't until this moment of taking complete responsibility for my contributions to those problems that my communication became more conscious. From this point on, I was able to connect with people more freely, more intimately, and more lovingly.

This shift came from one decision that drew from my answers to these questions: Do I want to take responsibility for how I'm creating disconnection and conflict in my relationships? Do I want to stop blaming others for my feelings, triggers, and reactions?

In our relationships with partners or dear friends, there is always a moment when we can step out of a negative loop—a moment when instead of getting drawn into a fight, we turn to loving curiosity.

In a call I had with a client, Paul, he shared how this awareness changed his marriage with his wife, Jennifer.

"Andy," he said, "I have to share something that just became clear to me. I was running, and it shot through my body like a lightning bolt. We cannot control others. We can only control how we react to others."

"Yes," I responded, "we discussed this for years. What makes it different now?"

He said, "I guess I could say that I feel it in my body. When I have been triggered by Jennifer, I knew logically that it was my issue, but I could not separate that out. It came out as blame to her even if I knew better."

I answered, "I guess you would have needed to make some peace inside of yourself to get to that point."

"Yes," he said. "I see that my nervous system is a bit more relaxed. I'm no longer listening with the anticipation that I will need to defend or feel a sense of shame."

"That's beautiful. So how does that translate back into the relationship?" I asked.

"I'm just taking responsibility for my own feelings and addressing the behaviors that I observe that do not work for me, without blame, and there is a lot of spaciousness."

"If you had to put into words what life was before and after, what would that sound like?"

"Before, I blamed Jennifer for how she made me feel. Now I observe how I feel. The feelings are still there. They just don't drive me anymore."

"How does life feel from there?"

"I feel like a grown-up for the first time," he said. "It feels like I can take responsibility for my own life."

I should note that I've been working with Paul for five years. I state this for readers who may blame themselves for not being able to reach the same state sooner, or for coaches who believe that fundamental changes must happen overnight. Personal responsibility is a journey. Once we accept that we are going to take personal responsibility, we are venturing into a dense forest without clear directions, just a dedication to finding our way out. The compass is love.

How does love guide my actions and reactions? How does it make sense of the actions of another? Personal responsibility requires dedication to looking at life through the lens of love. What that means in real terms is acknowledging that there are no bad people, just people who sometimes do bad things. Or stated another way, I do not make interpretations around another person's intentions; I simply observe their actions and see how they make me feel and address that as soon as I feel uncomfortable. I refuse to tell stories that vilify them and turn myself into a victim.

As mentioned already, personal responsibility starts with self-love. The concept of "love" can perhaps feel intangible. Let me make it concrete by using five examples of how life looks very different when we look at a situation through the lens of love:

Judgment: "My father is selfish and only thinks of himself."
Love: "How much pain must he have gone through to protect himself this way?"

Judgment: "She is disrespectful because she is always late."

Love: "She does not seem to realize how her being late is impacting us."

Judgment: "He is irresponsible and never does the chores."

Love: "It clearly is not easy for him to focus and get these things done."

Judgment: "He is not a good friend. I'm always the one making plans to meet."

Love: "I'm happy he's taking care of himself."

Judgment: "She is a child. She needs to grow up."

Love: "Apparently, she is comfortable living this way. I see that it makes me uncomfortable."

All these examples point out moments in our lives when we take personal responsibility by not blaming others for how they make us feel. Now, you might ask, "Are you telling me that you accept all these behaviors and use love as the justification for that?"

The answer is a resounding no. People often think that to love someone implies that we accept their behaviors. Nothing could be further from the truth. Simply, I am far more able to address any discomfort in the moment because I am not constricted in myself. I am not judging the other or myself, so there is a lot of space to address the issues in the moment.

To give an idea of how that would look, let's look again at all of the examples above and show how an actual response from love might look:

Judgment: "My father is selfish and only thinks of himself."

Love: "How much pain must he have gone through to protect himself this way?"

Love-Based Response: "Dad, I love that you take care of yourself by making decisions that suit your needs [observation]. Unfortunately, this decision does not work for me."

Judgment: "She is disrespectful because she is always late."
Love: "She does not seem to realize how her being late is impacting us."
Love-Based Response: "Sarah, I see that you are coming into the meeting after we start [observation]. This throws us off because we need to start over when you arrive. How can we shift this going forward?"

Judgment: "He is irresponsible and never does the chores."
Love: "It clearly is not easy for him to focus and get these things done."
Love-Based Response: "John, I see that you have not done your chores for several weeks now [observation]. This will need to change. How would you like to start organizing yourself so I do not need to manage you anymore?"

Judgment: "He is not a good friend. I'm always the one making plans to meet."
Love: "I'm happy he's taking care of himself."
Love-Based Response: "Steve, I know you are busy and plan everything at the last moment [observation]. I would love it if you'd sometimes call me to make plans."

Judgment: "She is a child. She needs to grow up."

Love: "Apparently, she is comfortable living this way. I see that it makes me uncomfortable."

Love-Based Response: "I admire your free spirit and sometimes see where I have lost it in myself when we are together [observation of SELF]. There are times when I see it goes too far for me, and I would like to discuss that if you're open to it."

I hear the critic in my head saying, "Andy, it is not that easy. What happens when the person gets triggered by what you have said? What if you state it as an observation, but the person receives it as an attack?"

This is what I call taking it personally. The answer remains the same. We continue interacting through the lens of love. For example:

"I see that this has impacted you in a way I did not intend. I can point out what I observed, and we can see what I am missing."

"I'm very sorry this hurt you. Obviously, I shared this to bring us closer, which apparently failed. I'm sorry for that. I'd love to see how we could get clarity around this."

"I must admit that I did not expect that reaction. I thought it could bring us closer, but that was clearly off the mark. What's going on inside you at the moment?"

In all of the examples above, we are creating more space for clarity to emerge. When taking personal responsibility, we are not defending a point or trying to be understood. We are allowing things to unfold in a way that suits both parties.

Sometimes it will get heated before things settle down. That's fine. Our objective is not to decide how we get clarity, only that we will continue until the clarity emerges. I call this "making space."

Although I make space, it does not mean that I surrender my wants and needs. I just don't force them if there is no space to have a dialogue. Sometimes we need to make space for the trigger that arises. When those triggers are defused, we can come back together.

When discussing this approach with very results-oriented people, I have been told, "Yes, Andy, but it takes too much time!" I cannot argue that in the moment, it will feel as if it takes more time, as we are not following the pattern we are most accustomed to: saying what we want and getting into an argument. But in the long run, a love-based approach is the quickest way to get to an outcome that works for both parties.

And to be clear, the outcome will not always be that we get what we want. The issue will simply be resolved quicker, with less drama. Taking personal responsibility means that we allow love to guide us, and we accept any outcome as long as it works for both parties.

✳ ✳ ✳

Lesson: Personal responsibility means seeing the world through the lens of love.

Exercise 10: Lens of Love

In this chapter, we looked at several scenarios through the lens of negative judgment or love. Try to translate the following statements from judgment to love. See how you'd experience the exact same situation differently if you flipped your lens to love.

ϟ Judgement ϟ	♡ Love ♡
He is so disrespectful.	He does not appear to see the consequences of his actions.
She is a liar.	She has said things many times that do not match what I see as reality.
He is lazy.	He is comfortable sitting around all day. That's not easy for me.
I don't like him.	
She is a drama queen.	
They are impolite.	
What a jerk.	

Reflecting on your answers, you may have found it difficult to see a person through the lens of love when you've previously judged them. Don't worry: it can be very challenging. And yet dedication to seeing people through this lens has a massive impact on how we interact and, in turn, how we experience the world around us. Give it a try, and you will find that life becomes lighter, and the people you interact with will appreciate you for it.

CHAPTER 11

Loving Me to Love You

I'm working with a couple, and the wife exclaims to the husband, "Why are you always correcting me? Why don't you look at your own shit?"

He looks at me helplessly, hoping I can turn the *Titanic*. "Andy, you see what I mean? I can't say anything without her getting triggered."

I pause and look at them both. I ask her, "What comes up when you feel judged by him?"

"I feel that he is looking down on me. Like he's demonstrating his superiority. I'm sick of it."

"I understand that. But help me understand, what is going on? You could just laugh at him and leave it at that, but you are fighting. What's going on?"

"I have never been accepted for me. I've always had to prove myself. From my father down. I am tired of being told what I don't know. It's exhausting. I just want to be accepted for me."

"And what if you did not need him, your father, or even me to accept you?"

She takes a deep breath. "That would mean I'd have to accept and love myself," she says, surprised as the words come out of her mouth. "That's not easy."

"I know, but how would this situation change if you simply loved yourself?"

"I would smile at you both and tell you to shut up and leave me alone so I could enjoy my own company."

Fully accepting ourselves is one of the hardest things any of us can do. Yet if we are unable to do so, our lack of self-acceptance will show up in all aspects of our relationships with ourselves and others.

The reason for this is obvious: How can we truly see and connect with ourselves when we believe that we aren't good enough as we are and that we should be different? And if we can't give ourselves self-acceptance, how can we accept others? Think how uncomfortable it is to sit with the feelings of shame and guilt in yourself, and then think how challenging it would be to be there for others who are feeling that way. In my experience, we tend to be reactive to these people because their issues are a reminder of what we have not made peace with in ourselves. In short, the less accepting we are of ourselves, the more disconnected we are from ourselves and others. Therefore, self-acceptance is one of the most fundamental ingredients for connection.

Unfortunately, the personal development industry often fails us in this regard. In personal development, people seek deeply-rooted beliefs and then try to change them. For instance, the belief "I am not worthy of love" is twisted into "I am worthy of love," which is repeated over and over again as a mantra. In my experience, this process actually creates more resistance, and therefore more confusion and pain, within oneself. I have found that absolute acceptance is the easiest, most effective way to change anything in myself—although, ironically, my intention is not to change anything at all.

There's a tool I use for cultivating self-acceptance of everything I resist in myself; I briefly demonstrated this method in Chapter 8. I dig deep until I find the thing that hurts the most to say out loud. I say that thing out loud, followed by, "and it's okay." For example, when I feel helpless in a situation, I can say, "I am helpless, and it's okay." I apply it to situations where I have experienced pain from other people. "My father never accepted me, and it's okay." I also apply it to my own shortcomings and mistakes. "I'm selfish, and it's okay."

Over the years, I've used this tool consistently to accept uncomfortable or painful experiences, deeply-rooted beliefs, things

I dislike about myself. In this way, I find peace without needing to change or fix anything. If I learn to completely accept something I'm resisting, it's no longer a problem. And when it's not a problem, it holds no power over me. I can simply observe experiences, thoughts, and feelings without reacting to them.

Over time, I've fine-tuned the method to make it even stronger and more effective. I've learned that sometimes when I simply say, "It's okay," I can still stay stuck in my resistance. I am giving the emotion a place, but I'm also keeping it in check. It feels as if I am trying to convince myself that it is okay, even though on some level I feel it is not. It is another coping mechanism. How would it feel to completely redefine the thought?

Instead of saying, "It's okay," I now use something stronger: "It's fucking great." With something from a client like, "I hate my parents, and it's okay," I take it to the next level and have them say, "I hate my parents, and it's fucking great. It's fantastic. It's wonderful." It creates a strange paradox, but it works. Using the stronger version somehow gives me a freedom to let go of any ideas I hold about myself. It helps me to *completely* embrace the thing I am resisting. Now the thing I have resisted gives me joy.

With this stronger addition to the method, I am no longer managing the emotion. I am no longer pacifying the feeling I'm resisting. I am simply embracing it to the point that it loses its stranglehold over my thinking. I decide that, moving forward, I will no longer manage my thinking with techniques. I am ready to explore another level of self-acceptance. In fact, it is much greater than self-acceptance: self-love.

What does life look like if we love every part of ourselves? If we enjoy the judgment cast upon us by others? If we laugh at every thought that does not serve us? If we decide to see everything that constrains us as "fucking great" and we're free? It's radical to take over a thought that's dominated us and destroy it in one fell swoop. That thought may still come up, but there's no longer a negative reaction to it. There's no longer a need to defend. It disappears as quickly as it came.

Try this for yourself. What are the things in yourself that you resist the most? What traumas have happened to you that have damaged you the most? Find those things, and then state them out loud. When I say out loud, I really mean it. Don't just say it in your mind, or whisper it, or state it without emotion. Fully feel the words as they come out of your mouth. Don't sugarcoat. Say the things that are the most painful to say out loud. The things that feel like a piece of your heart is torn out when the words come out of your mouth.

"My mother never loved me."

"My father was an abusive alcoholic."

"I don't know if I can stay married."

"I don't love my partner."

You know you are in the right ballpark when you feel your body vibrate. If you are not in tune with that way of feeling yourself, then use your logic. Say, "If I said that, wow, that would be painful." And there is always something. Don't go fooling yourself and jump over this moment by convincing yourself that you are beyond this.

Now that you've spoken this horrible thought out loud, follow it with "and it's okay." Repeat the phrase five to ten times, and you will find that it begins to settle.

You are telling yourself a lie so you can experience a deeper truth. Nothing in this makes sense. Nor should it. This is an incredible way to trick your brain into an experience—an experience it will reject outright if you give it a chance. Don't let it. Repeat the statement until you feel a calm come over you, somewhere between a tear and a laugh.

Once you have made the "and it's okay" statement, then you can graduate to the next level of absurdity. Take the thought you've made peace with and go one step further. Say the thing you judge/hate/fear/shame yourself for and add, "And it's fucking great." It's excellent. It's incredible. It's beautiful.

You will probably feel your entire body resist. That's to be expected. And yet in saying it out loud and making peace with it, it changes forever.

"I am [the thing I'm most ashamed of], and it's fucking great. It's wonderful."

Say that ten times over, and with each repetition, you will feel a softness come over the thought. A space develops where there was once resistance. In the end, you will say, "I feel different, but I can't exactly say why." To paraphrase Newton, for every energy, there is an equal and opposite energy. By embracing this thought, you have removed the latent energy of resistance and replaced it with love and acceptance.

Our brain produces thoughts. Most of the time, we have no ability to control thoughts. Once repressed, they come back again and again. When we are tired and weak. When we are angry and frustrated. In our dreams. It goes back to the old adage, "Don't think of a pink elephant." The surest way to think of something is to tell ourselves not to think it. If we tell ourselves, "Don't think about how your parents treated you," we are in fact inviting that thought to linger on. It will continue to haunt us in different shapes and forms.

Embracing our worst thoughts does not mean they will no longer come into our minds. It simply means that they will be given the same value as any other thought that carries no weight.

It's not enough to accept something as "just okay," because we're still beholden to push back and manage it. When the thought arises, we give it time and effort. By saying it more strongly, we trick our brain into letting go of a thought completely so that it doesn't define us in any way. As the common phrase goes, "That which we resist persists." It's only through acceptance that we can make peace with the beliefs, thoughts, and experiences that control our lives.

Lesson: We love ourselves so that we can love others.

Exercise 11: 100% Self-Love

Following up from the exercise described in this chapter, here are a few questions that will support you in nurturing self-love:

What's something that's been challenging to accept about yourself or your life?

If you had to phrase this one thing in a sentence that feels deeply emotional, what would that sentence be? For example: "My father never loved me," "I am worthless," "No one cares about me," "I'm an imposter," etc.

As an experiment, take that sentence and add, "And it's okay" to the end. For example: "No one has ever loved me, and it's okay."

Repeat this sentence five times out loud. Speak it slowly, taking a breath and leaving space between each repetition. As you speak the sentence, feel into what moves inside you. For added impact, find someone you're comfortable with and look them in the eyes as you speak. Make sure to tell them it is an exercise and that they are not to say anything.

AND THAT'S OKAY.
AND THAT'S OKAY.
AND THAT'S OKAY.
AND THAT'S OKAY.
AND THAT'S OKAY.

Take a deep breath between repetitions and allow your body to feel the words as they pass through you. Remember, you are not convincing yourself; rather, you are allowing yourself to feel the deeper truth behind these words.

Take a moment to write down anything that you noticed or discovered while doing the exercise.

RECAP

I hope that you were able to create some love for yourself through this exercise. This work was made popular by my friend Peter Koenig, who uses people's relationship with money as a means of self-discovery and an opportunity to embrace what we resist inside of ourselves. It may not have been easy; maybe you heard your internal voice say, "It's *not* okay!" In this exercise, we are telling ourselves a lie so we can feel a deeper truth. If it does not land for you, then don't sweat it. In fact, in that case, I would use the same tool: "This exercise did not work for me, and that's okay."

CHAPTER 12

Repossessing Your Agency

A core theme that has come up again and again in my writing is the word "agency," meaning the agency that one has over their decision-making and life. My mentor, Cees de Bruin, would often point out that people have less agency over their lives than they might imagine. He often said, "People are very much a byproduct of their environment, blind to their reactive nature."

To prove this point, he'd ask, "Do you believe you have control over your own thoughts?" He would follow this question with a thought experiment, asking people, "Try to think of a thought before you think it." Take a moment and try this for yourself. Observe your thoughts as they come into your mind and feel where they are coming from. Now bring your attention to that thought. Did you decide to think that thought? If not, where did it come from?

His point was both simple and transformative. Thoughts are generated in the dark recesses of our brain. As with a rolling bingo cage that spits out numbers, we do not decide what thoughts arise.

I like to think of my brain as a computer that generates thoughts for which I am not responsible, not unlike being with a friend who might behave awkwardly in public. "Yes, I'm standing next to him, but he is not a reflection of me." What we can decide is what to do with those thoughts when they do arise. The word most often used to describe the ability to observe our thoughts without attachment is mindfulness.

If we are completely honest with ourselves, then we would acknowledge that much of what we think is agency is just a deep desire to believe we have free will. We are not the independent thinkers we might believe ourselves to be. We have an operating system that runs without our conscious awareness. For the most part, we just use the applications that run on the operating system, which we barely give any thought. And yet the operating system is the basis for everything. If that does not exist, the applications don't run.

I am often accused of making things too abstract, so let's endeavor to illustrate this topic with a story.

My friend Joseph always talks about his thoughts. When I am with Joseph, he will jump from one topic to the next. Whatever pops into his mind is not qualified by its relevance but rather automatically assumed as all-important: "I was thinking that I am not living my full potential"; "I think I should be more focused"; "I am not sure about my relationship." You get the picture.

Although I love Joseph, it can be exhausting to spend time with him. We all have "that friend." What we see in Joseph is a lack of awareness that he is not his thoughts—i.e., just because we have a thought does not make it important. If we are unable to separate ourselves from our thoughts, we can easily get stuck in a loop where we live at the whim of what comes up.

That is the challenge we face in our development: the balance between knowing what we know and at the same time acknowledging that we are subject to an operating system that's hardwired to see things a certain way and has limitations.

This goes back to what Karl Popper said, that there is no universal, objective truth because each person creates truth for themselves. Each person makes a statement and then decides the context in which that statement is true. If we limit the context, we can make just about any statement true. I want to reiterate that this is not a means of making truth arbitrary. Far from it. We are staying open to all possibilities and thereby remaining in a constant state of wonder and learning.

The gift that this understanding allows us is the power of questions. When I let go of the need to be "right," I begin to understand that the other person has a context that they are speaking from that I have yet to understand. The mind turns from thinking it knows to wondering what it does not know.

Recently, I was with a client who told me that she was fighting with her partner. She shared, "I spent an hour sitting quietly as he spoke, and then he tells me, 'You're not listening.' I was hurt and wanted to defend. Then I thought of you and decided that I was not going to react from pain."

"What did you do?"

"I told him I was sorry. I did not try to explain or justify all the thoughts that were coming up in my head. It felt like I was no longer fighting my urge to be seen and heard."

"And then what?"

"Actually, through his talking, he worked it out for himself and later apologized to me for not hearing or seeing me. Amazingly, all I did was remain quiet and not take the thoughts seriously. I created space for wonder."

In the place of not knowing is where dialogue emerges. I use the word "dialogue" to point out a moment where two people meet in mutual understanding. It's not a debate to see who's right or to win but rather a surrender to seeing one another. As we know, this state can be very challenging to find when people carry strong opinions or feel the need to be seen—especially when a person with his own limiting context for truth perceives limitations in the context the other person has chosen to use.

I've often found that believing we can "win" an argument leads to vigorous discussion and further alienation. If a conversation is an argument and not a dialogue, I choose not to spend much time with it. The reason is quite simple. If a person is not reflecting on his or her own beliefs, or at least allowing a suspension of them for a moment, then there is a goal orientation to the interaction that draws away from connection. Don't get me wrong. I love getting to know a person's understanding, and I ask a lot of questions when a subject interests me. But when I see a person needs me to agree with their opinion so that they feel a sense of peace or accomplishment, I slowly transition away from the interaction.

What I've learned is that everyone gets to decide the context in which they see the world and ignore the context that does not suit their narrative. This is often referred to as "living in an echo chamber." If we are unaware that we are living in an echo chamber, we are blind to the fact that we are setting our mind up to be in a constant state of attack or defense. This uncomfortable state requires an enemy. And if we track back the ideas that we are defending, many of them did not even come from our firsthand experience but rather came from the word of another.

When we allow our psyche to be influenced by a constant barrage of one-sided media outlets, we slowly shift from ideas to ideologies—fixed ways of seeing the world. This way of living is terribly confining and leaves little room for deeper understanding of ourselves and the world around us. We lose agency over our own thinking by allowing it to be taken over, usually unconsciously, by a belief system disguised as an independent media outlet.

The point of all this is that when we understand the limits of agency in ourselves and others, we can look past that idea to more easily connect with others. In Chapter 1, I gave the equation that beliefs lead to thoughts, which in turn determine behavior. When we observe people's behavior, it's relatively easy to trace it back to their belief system. For example, when someone says, "I think" before making a statement, I immediately tune in to how I myself feel when I say this. Sometimes we use it to express a general uncertainty. At other times, it's used to acknowledge that everyone has their own "truth," so the person is simply stating his or her own. "I think" may even be evidence of arrogance when making a strong statement. So, of course, we need to tune in to the intentions with which the words are spoken. And with that intention (what we see as behavior), we can tell a lot about a person's beliefs.

Let's say a person is with a group of people who are all trying to make a group decision and sharing their opinions. She raises her voice with a hint of frustration and says, "I think it's best for us to finally just decide." We know that she is likely getting impatient. She believes the decision-making process is taking too long. She also believes that raising her voice in exhaustion may push the group to act.

We could say, "Well, that's just stating the obvious." But then we miss out on all the things that could possibly be seen about this person. (Of course, we're making many assumptions. But it's okay as long as we're conscious of that.) What might we be able to assume or conjecture about this person's beliefs? We could say that a person who gets frustrated with a group process possibly believes that getting things done in a group is tiresome and unproductive. Also, time is being wasted. Or maybe they believe one person is at the heart of the delay.

All these beliefs will show up not only in this one meeting but also in all aspects of her life. If we are considering her for a leadership role, it's easy to see how her beliefs might translate into that role when patience is required. For instance, working as a coach or facilitating group activities could be a challenge.

This is the process I use when interviewing candidates for any role. I spend very little time thinking if he or she is qualified based on skills and much more time thinking how his or her behavior will translate into the role as it has been laid out. This is not an exact science, but there are many key behavioral indicators that give clues into a person's beliefs.

One of the biggest of these indicators is defensiveness. When a person is triggered and begins defending themselves early in a discussion, this suggests that they are insecure or possibly lack confidence. This is often tied to a low degree of self-acceptance. Interestingly, people with low self-acceptance are often high performers because they have something to prove. It's not hard to see how the relationship with an unaccepting parent is often behind this insecurity and need to prove oneself. In my own life, I have the voice of my father telling me, "You will never amount to anything," and I see an immediate drive to prove myself.

How does knowing all this translate back into our relationships with partners and dear friends? As we observe the behavior of others, instead of judging, we can ask ourselves, "How do I feel inside when I behave that way?" I don't try to interpret their feelings. Instead, I try to sense where their behavior exists within me. This generates compassion, and when I operate from compassion, it's harder to judge. I'm now less capable of separating myself from the other. I see the other as part of me and therefore a mirror to myself.

In the moments where I am unable to find compassion for others, there is often a part of myself that I have not fully accepted. This hearkens back to my self-acceptance practice, where I state out loud what's hardest to admit or make peace with in myself and follow it with "and it's fucking great."

As I write this now, I could say, "I'm worried that in being so honest about how I see the world, I will be judged as callous and arrogant, and that's fucking great." In making peace with this statement, I immediately have compassion for the challenges of people who may be judging me. I know how hard it is to be around people who I have perceived as callous and arrogant, especially when I am insecure. Our ability to find compassion for others is directly related to our ability to love that same thing in ourselves.

This idea that we have "agency" over all of our actions may seem empowering. In reality, this inflated sense of confidence can actually create disconnection and alienation. If we believe that we all have power to choose and that our choices are always conscious, it becomes easy to judge ourselves and others for making "wrong" choices. However, when we understand how much of our reactions simply come from unseen programming, we can have much greater compassion for ourselves and others.

＊＊＊

Lesson: We can control our reactions, not our thoughts.

Exercise 12: Popcorn Thoughts

A lot of this chapter was dedicated to discussing how thoughts pop into our heads and impact our psyches. If you have practiced mindfulness in the past, then listening to your thoughts may not be new to you. Here we are going to take a few minutes to touch the inception of a thought. For this exercise, find a quiet space.

We begin by listening to our thoughts. Take a moment. Close your eyes and take three deep breaths. With this quiet mind, begin to see the activity of your brain. Pay attention to how it wanders, the thoughts that come up, and any judgment that may arise. Set an alarm for five minutes. Return here afterward.

What did you observe?

_____

_____

_____

How did you see yourself reacting when the thoughts popped up?

_____

_____

_____

How did it feel to observe your thoughts from this space?

_____

_____

_____

What realization or discoveries did you make?

_____

_____

_____

Were you able to think a thought before you thought it? (This is a trick question.)

_____

_____

_____

This exercise may have been challenging for you. Quieting the mind is not a simple thing, and it is easy to get distracted. Yet in this space of surrendering to our thoughts and observing them, as opposed to reacting to them, we can begin to navigate life with more grace and less reactivity. Consider how many thoughts pop up that are outside of your control. What would happen to you if you took all those thoughts seriously? Your head would be a noisy, chaotic place.

CHAPTER 13

Personal Affront

"If she is perceived as incompetent, the investors will not be comfortable putting more money in," I say calmly.

He jumps out of his chair and shouts, "Are you saying that my wife is incompetent!"

"No," I clarify. "I said that if the investors feel that she cannot competently act, they are not going to be comfortable investing more money."

He now stands above me, eyes raging, ready to fight. "Apologize to my wife. No one calls my wife incompetent."

I slowly get up from the table, pack my bags, and leave. I can tell that he has taken things so personally and is so triggered that there is no reasoning with him.

We've all heard or said the phrase, "Why are you taking this so personally?" We might have an intuitive sense of what that means, but understanding this distinction is very important when it comes to navigating our relationships with others. And unfortunately, we are often unaware of what makes things personal and why. This lack of awareness makes us prone to making things personal.

When we take something personally, it is always tied to a belief we have about ourselves. Take for example the belief that I am a polite person. If for some reason I am told, "You're rude," it's highly likely that I will become defensive and respond, "No, I'm not!" This is an example of taking something personally. If I were to say, "What makes you say that?" I'd be taking it less personally.

We recognize when someone is taking something personally because they get defensive. Their body tightens. The tone of their voice changes. They react more quickly. The personal is often reflected in blame: "But you are the same," or, "I'm that way because of you." The more we blame others for our feelings and problems, the more trapped we are in the personal. In these personal reactions, we *are* our thoughts. When we begin to observe our thoughts and reactions, we take things less personally.

You're possibly familiar with the distinction between reacting and responding. When we react to a thought, we are not seeing how that thought affects us. It is an unseen part of our identity. We are therefore inescapably attached to the thought and unable to do anything but react to it. Usually, our reactions happen so quickly that we're unaware of them. We are our thoughts and our triggers.

Many self-help and relationship books tell us how to navigate difficult moments when we encounter them. It's even been done in this book at times. But being told how to do something does not address the emotional challenges. I may tell you to not react defensively and to respond with curiosity instead, which sounds great in theory, but in the middle of a trigger, all that great advice flies out the window.

Of course, it would be ideal if this were a skill—something that could be memorized and practiced. Unfortunately, this is less of a skill and more of an awareness. To better understand this, we can start by sensing how we react when we are triggered and take things personally. We feel it in our bodies. I personally feel my head fill with a gray, confused anger that occupies it like a fog. My jaw and chest tighten. If you look inside yourself, there may be very different reactions. If you have trouble seeing yourself in this way, it may be easier to notice personal reactions in others.

Now imagine a situation where two people are unaware of how they have made a subject personal. This state is recognizable through the use of labels like "lazy," "racist," "liar," or "creep." Once things turn personal, it becomes clear that people are stuck in a negative reinforcing loop. And as pointed out, those loops crop up frequently.

The big question is, what happens when one of us can step out of this dynamic? How does the interaction change when one person shifts from reacting to observing their thoughts as a third person, almost as if they were watching two other people have a discussion? This is what is meant by making things impersonal.

The more we're able to treat our thoughts as if they are just another observation, the less personally we take things. Think of someone with whom you've had frequent conflict. Imagine being a third person in the room, observing the two of you argue. That's the space of the impersonal.

The more personally we take things ourselves, and the more personal we make things for others, the more conflict we will have in our relationships. Communicating and responding from a more impersonal space requires learning both how to stop taking things personally and how to stop triggering the personal in others by how we phrase things.

An easy way to recognize the personal in conversations is by the use of "you."

A wife is frustrated because her husband didn't take the trash out. Consider the differences between these two approaches:

- "You said you would do it, and you didn't."
- "I saw it wasn't done. What happened?"

We see a very different energy between these two statements. In the first instance, she is inviting her husband to turn defensive. In the second, she is inviting him to reflect. Which one do you think is less likely to end in an argument?

The key lies in observation. Observations are the things we see rather than interpret. "The trash is inside" is a statement. If we say, "You did not take the trash out," it's also a statement, but it asks the other to defend him or herself. How we phrase our questions determines how personal they come across to others.

Even more important than the words we use is the intention behind them. One might appear to state something in observational terms but have a tainted intention behind it. This is best seen in the word "why." If I ask, "Why didn't you take the trash out?" with the intention of blaming or shaming the other, then it will be heard in my voice. In fact, the word "why" will almost always be stressed.

Take the same sentence and remove any blame or shame, and we'll hear a compassionate question that is genuinely seeking to understand: "Why didn't you take the trash out?" We can almost hear the next sentence: "Is there anything wrong?" In this instance, we hear that the one speaking is not triggered. And in responding rather than reacting, he or she is creating more space to interact. This is at the heart of making things less personal. It increases the "talk-aboutable," meaning the things we can discuss in a relationship without triggering each other.

I use the example of taking out the trash because I know that anyone who has gone through such a situation will be screaming in their heads, "It's not that easy! I've told my partner several times, and he/she still refuses to do it."

The recommendation is to continue to keep it impersonal. "I know we've discussed this a few times already [observation], and I know that it tends to get missed [observation with a slight potential for defense]. What can we do to ensure it gets done in the future [invitation]?" In this phrasing, the speaker is allowing what might turn into judgment and animosity to remain observational and inviting.

If this attempt does not work, then we can persist in our request while continuing to keep it impersonal. "I must admit, I'm really getting frustrated [observation of an emotion] about this. We've discussed this on four different occasions now [observation], and I am not sure what to do next. I don't want to manage you, but it's what this is turning into [observation]."

And it continues from here.

It's important to note that I'm not explaining this because impersonal is always better. I've just found that the more we can work things out impersonally, the more things remain open and "talk-aboutable." I have also seen that expressing myself in anger is sometimes very powerful and necessary—especially when people are in denial and avoidance in areas where they are not taking responsibility and causing harm to others. I've been known to give a good yell, and that's also important and necessary.

The major difference between now and when I was in my thirties is that the anger feels more like a response and less like a reaction. Something is telling me that all other ways of interacting have not worked and this is my last shot to shift a behavior.

Someone reading that might say, "You still have space to develop," and that would also be true. And yet a good yell has achieved things that clearly worked out well. We get to decide how we choose to interact with the world, and we do not need to judge ourselves for getting angry.

In my relationship with Rani, I've experienced a recurring trigger. Whenever I share my enthusiasm about something, she feels the need to temper it for fear that I may lose my objectivity. A recent conversation went something like this:

Me: "I love this house, and I think it would be great to have a look. I've already been in contact with the seller, and it feels good."

Rani: "But you know you can't trust the seller. You do not know him. He could be a thief."

Me: "I know that. But it's nice to have contact with him. And so far, I believe he has answered my questions honestly."

Rani: "But if he is a good thief, then that is what he is trained to do: manipulate you."

Me: "I understand this. But in the fifteen years we've been together, have you seen me be a poor judge of character?"

Rani: "You bought that iPhone on the internet, and it was a scam."

Me: "I know, and as I told you at the time, I bought it through PayPal so I would not lose any money. I would not have bought it if I did not have the assurance of PayPal."

Rani: "You asked me if you have ever been scammed, and I answered your question."

In this conversation, I am not hearing Rani completely, as she is driven by risk aversion. If she feels even slightly that objectivity has been lost, she gets triggered. I, on the other hand, love the enthusiasm of the journey. I know that he could be a scammer, but at the same time, I also know that it is not easy for a scammer to keep his story straight if I ask questions and listen attentively. I often say, "I treat people with complete trust until they show me otherwise."

In the past, these conversations have felt like Rani was throwing a wet blanket on the fire of my enthusiasm. I've let her fears affect me and lost my passion to continue something. I had the narrative, "She is taking all the fun out of things." Now I slow things down and engage her where she is and not where I would prefer that she is, i.e., as excited as I am.

The conversation continued something like this:

Me: "Hey, babe, I see us falling into this pattern, and I want to make sure that we do not go down a path that pulls us away from this great opportunity."

Rani: "I just want you to acknowledge that this could be a scam."

Me: "Of course this could be a scam. But for this scam to work, then he would have had to make up a lot of facts that I have already checked. His mother died last year, and I see that this is corroborated on the internet. The house was purchased in 2004, which I can see on the deed. There will be no money transferred until the lawyer sets up a contract and does all of the due diligence. What else can we do so that you are comfortable that this is not a scam?"

Rani: "You do know that he could falsify details on the internet, right?"

Me: "That would be possible, but then he would also have to

falsify the documents of sale, which show that his mother died and left him the house. You are right; this could be an elaborate scam. But there is no indication that it is, and there is every indication that it is not. How comfortable are you proceeding given all this?"

Rani: "That feels like enough. I just don't want you to get so excited that you neglect the clues that this may be a scam."

Me: "I got that. I have been looking out for it from the start, and I keep feeling more confident, not less."

Rani: "Good."

In writing this example, I am also very aware that I did not ask Rani, "Where are these feelings coming from? How can I help you feel more relaxed in this process?" These questions may have led to a learning opportunity for both of us.

We always have the choice of how deep we want to take an interaction. I have decided not to turn my relationship into an extended therapy session. If both of us are happy continuing forward and the topic is not essential to our mutual well-being, then that is enough. If Rani does not have a question regarding her deep need to mitigate risk and how that might impact those around her, I do not try to teach or convince. I did that for many years, and it did not end well.

Now I just make sure that she feels seen and heard and that I am taking her fears into account. In the past, such discussions would have led us to a day of shutdown and resentment. Now they are cleared up within minutes, and we continue as we were.

✳ ✳ ✳

Lesson: Once I label you, I'm making it personal.

Exercise 13: Label You

Knowing when you begin to take things personally is critical to maintaining healthy relationships. You can spot this either in your body or through the words you are using to describe another. In these moments, it's important to slow down. Labels are not problematic in and of themselves. They become issues when we use an implied negative meaning or a stereotype to demonize another.

Look at the following labels in the left-hand column. There are two columns to the right: "Personal" and "Impersonal." Show how the given label can be made personal or impersonal in a short text. Observe how the personal column has the potential to demonize.

LABEL	PERSONAL	IMPERSONAL
He's a liberal.	He is pro-abortion.	He holds liberal values.
She's a conservative.	She is pro-gun.	She holds conservative values.
He's privileged.	He was given everything.	He had opportunities other did not.
They are anti-vaxxers.		
They are one-percenters.		
He's uneducated.		
He's unprofessional.		
She's shallow.		

Labeling is our subtle or not so subtle way of demonizing another. As soon as we make the disagreement personal, it is very hard to see another person. We force them to retreat or attack and then use that behavior to demonize them further. In making the discussion personal, we fall into a trap where, in the end, both parties lose. The start of the healing journey begins when we no longer use a label to separate but instead ask the simple question, "What makes you say that?"

CHAPTER 14

Impersonally Personal

One of my struggles in writing a book like this is that there are exceptions to everything. In this case, the exception is important enough to take up an entire chapter.

As I've aged, I've realized more and more how paradoxes are present in the most important lessons in life. In the world of the personal, the paradox is this: in order to make things less personal (reactive), we must make them personal (vulnerable). Stated another way, unless we show ourselves in vulnerability, the other has no chance to really see us.

I think of my own childhood. When I was nineteen years old, my mother was hit and killed by a drunk driver. I shut down emotionally. I was in deep pain, but I showed it to no one. I avoided discussions where it might come up. Since I was unable to show my emotion, I did not give anyone the chance to truly see me. Of course, there were people who could see my suffering, but it was not because I shared it.

I deeply wanted to be seen and supported but was unable to ask for those things. The consequence was that I became resentful. I was not showing myself and at the same time blaming others for not showing themselves to me. Therefore, it was easy for others to judge me and my actions. How could they do otherwise?

This is an extreme example. But a similar dynamic occurs regularly in relationships where people are hurt or disappointed and are unable to share their feelings. Hiding this in a relationship means that we are showing the less vulnerable part of how we are feeling, thereby making the conversation more likely to become personal and to trigger others.

So again, in order to make a conversation less personal, we need to show more of ourselves. And it could be argued that there are layers, each becoming more vulnerable and making it easier for others to see us. Consider this example of starting with the personal, then moving into deeper levels of vulnerability:

"You are a jerk."

"I'm angry with you."

"What you did made me angry."

"I'm uncomfortable, and I need to talk."

"I'm feeling helpless."

These levels of vulnerability each show varying degrees of allowing ourselves to be seen. The more vulnerable we become, the more we move away from "You are" statements and toward "I'm feeling" statements.

But it's not just about using the words. At times, when people are asked to state things using "I feel" statements, they contort themselves inauthentically to say it "right." The other person might then react to what he or she feels from the undercurrent of how it's said.

In one such training, I witnessed a teacher endeavoring to instruct a struggling couple. The wife told the husband, "You don't think of me in the mornings when we are getting the kids ready for school. I'm the one making sure that they get out on time."

The teacher interrupted and said, "Can you say the same sentence, but this time, start with 'I feel'? Instead of telling him what he is doing wrong, tell him how it makes you feel."

The wife tried again. "I feel like you leave me to do all the work in the morning and now I am taking care of three kids instead of two."

The intention of the trainer was for the wife to show some

vulnerability as to how she was being impacted by his behavior so that her husband could have a better understanding and empathize. Instead of the statement being about what he was doing, it would be about how she was being impacted by him. But the point was missed in this exercise.

If we reflect back on the last two chapters, this intention has been addressed over and over again. The challenge remains that unless we have the insight to know why we behave as we do, then whatever behavioral changes we make are based on skill, not awareness. And it's important to note that rephrasing a sentence without changing the intention behind it will not bring us much further. In order to touch the core of the difference, we require vulnerability.

When I suggest using "I feel" statements, I'm building on the lessons so far in this book, based on the understanding that the person using the "I feel" statement is always part of the dynamic that is going wrong. This person is missing something, and they can take responsibility by showing how another's actions affect them. By doing this, the dynamic is more likely to become positive, so the only thing stopping an individual is themselves.

I see this challenge show up in many of the leaders I coach. They often hold the idea that if they don't know the answer to a question, it's best to say as little as possible. In some ways, this makes sense. Who wants to talk about something they don't understand? Yet, like everything in life, both actions and nonactions have consequences. In this case, when leaders don't share their uncertainty, it often results in built-up frustration and resentment among their team members, to the tune of, "She never makes decisions," or, "He is avoidant."

In one case, someone I was coaching was delaying a decision to share the company vision. It had taken a long time to create, and he was not confident in what had been produced. In meeting after meeting he was asked, "When are you going to deliver the vision?"

He grew nervous and avoidant as his inability to finish began weighing on him.

I asked him, "What stops you from sharing your struggle with the group?"

He responded, "It's not their responsibility. It's mine."

"That might be so," I acknowledged. "But if you share your challenge, at least they will understand the delay and possibly be able to support you. Whatever the consequence, at least they will not blame you for being lazy or whatever other stories they may be writing."

After a bit of back and forth, he agreed to share his dilemma with the group. I asked him to share not only why he was delaying but also the emotional toll it was taking on him.

He went into the meeting a bit nervous and said, "I know that many of you have been waiting on the vision, and I must admit that it has not been easy for me. Although I have been working on it for weeks now, I am not comfortable with how it has been going. I see that I did not communicate that well. I was not sure exactly how to proceed, so I have been delaying the release. I've been hoping that inspiration would hit me, but it has not. I share all this so that you can better understand the challenges I have been facing and be up front about it."

As he shared this, he was flooded with emotional support from his team. People rallied around him. As a consequence of that meeting, a group was formed to develop the vision together—the very thing the man wanted but wasn't exactly sure how to achieve.

I spoke with him afterward, and he said, "It's amazing how by avoiding sharing the thing that is most challenging, we are not giving others the possibility to support us there. I thought I needed to do it all on my own, which was exactly the thing that stopped me from sharing where I was at and getting the benefit of the group. It's so obvious and yet so difficult at times."

I shared, "It's exactly in the moments we feel weakest that it's hardest to show how uncomfortable we are feeling. When we need support, we often pretend that we don't. If people don't see what's going on behind the scenes in our mind, they don't really know how to help or simply calm their doubts or insecurities. What I have learned is that in this state, we tend to blame others for not seeing us, even though we are not showing ourselves."

This is a business example, but it is equally true in personal relationships. Assuming there is mutual trust and respect in the relationship, by sharing more of ourselves in being personal and vulnerable, we are less likely to trigger defensiveness in the other and can more easily keep difficult conversations impersonal and connected.

Lesson: Vulnerability makes it less personal.

Exercise 14: Five Steps Down

The focus of this chapter has been understanding the nature of making things impersonal. To practice this, we will work to ever increasing levels of vulnerability by playing Five Steps Down. After each of the sentences listed below, I am going to ask you to share four additional sentences that progressively increase in vulnerability. If you have difficulty coming up with sentences on your own, don't worry. You can cheat and see the answers at the end of the book.

We can use the following example to start.

Lv.1	"You are a jerk."
Lv.2	"I'm angry with you."
Lv.3	"What you did made me angry."
Lv.4	"I'm uncomfortable, and I need to talk."
Lv.5	"I'm feeling helpless."

Lv.1	You're screwing up your life.
Lv.2	
Lv.3	
Lv.4	
Lv.5	

Lv.1	Your partner is terrible.
Lv.2	
Lv.3	
Lv.4	
Lv.5	

Lv.1	You are totally unreliable.
Lv.2	
Lv.3	
Lv.4	
Lv.5	

Lv.1 ↓	You are lazy.
Lv.2 ↓	
Lv.3 ↓	
Lv.4 ↓	
Lv.5	

(RECAP)

This chapter was all about the power of vulnerability and its potential to help people to see us. When people see us, they are less likely to make assumptions around our intentions because we have already made ourselves transparent. When we allow people to see behind the curtain of our insecurities and incapacities, we give them the chance to understand us. It is never guaranteed that they will meet us in this space, but we do not do this for them. We do it for ourselves. Being vulnerable is a dedication to surrendering to others' potential judgments of us, knowing that the alternative can be even more emotionally draining.

SECTION IV

Creating Context for Deeper Connection

CHAPTER 15

The Energy of Intention Speaks Volumes

Intention is the energy that is emitted and felt when interacting with another. Even if we use all the wrong words, people often feel our intentions, which gives a lot of space to miss the mark on how we word our questions. Or conversely, if we use all the right words but have a masked intention, that will often be felt as well.

Intention is really the essence of why we speak to begin with. If we had no intention, there would be no reason to speak. We would simply share space in silence. Each time we say something, there is an intention behind it. Are we giving advice because we believe the other person is making bad decisions? Are we frustrated with the way the other has treated someone and wanting him or her to understand that? Are we bored and want company? Are we lonely?

Although we can use words to hide behind, it's nearly impossible to hide intentions. We convince ourselves that we are there to help, but in the end, we can't hide that we're hiding. People feel it on a very subtle level. Even if we think we are aware of our intentions, more often than not, we are blind as can be. The urge to speak grows, and the words pop out:

"I think you should . . ."

"If I were you . . ."

"How about . . ."

Suppose I believe a friend is making bad decisions. If I want to pull from the lessons in the prior chapters, then I would first need to address the fact that "bad" implies judgment. To soften the blow to my friend's ego and come with a loving intention, I must first turn the word "bad" into an observation—something that can be discussed without assuming from the start that it is negative. I would describe the situation as follows: I see my friend has made some decisions that appear to have some negative consequences.

This is more than semantics or putting "lipstick on a pig" to make it more palatable. Stating my observation in this way demonstrates true understanding that although I believe there are negative consequences, that has yet to be seen. Quite possibly, the consequences are required in order for something new to emerge. In showing that my intentions are to explore and not to fix, my friend will be far more receptive to feedback and support. The reason for this is twofold: he will not feel judged, and he will see my openness to reflect with him.

When our intention is to fix someone because we think we know better, it bleeds into our interactions. The other feels it and will often react negatively.

It's also important to recognize that, for the most part, people don't feel as though they have bad intentions. People who commit the most horrible atrocities quite often feel that they have the best intentions. As crazy as it sounds, Hitler believed he was doing the world a service by exterminating Jews. In his mind, he was a great person. Which brings us to the saying, "The road to hell is paved with good intentions."

If everyone believes they are doing the right thing and we have several indications things are going wrong, it's not always easy to help. People who are not asking for help will feel pressured if we offer. And even if we are successful in helping them, the offer is often not appreciated or is met with resentment afterward. I have the battle scars to prove it.

For years, I went around telling people everything I thought they should know. A conversation early on in my relationship with Rani would look like this (as shown in previous chapters):

"I've heard this so many times. Why don't you do something about it," I would say with an undercurrent of agitation.

She'd reply, "I'm sure you have a point, but it's not that easy. I have other considerations."

"I know that. But what if you could learn how to change this for good? What if you looked into doing this course that is being offered?"

Such an interaction invariably led to tension and both of us shutting down emotionally. Although my intention was to help, I was not helping. I was trying to solve a problem that quite frankly I was not being asked to solve.

For this reason, as I've stated, I make my intentions very clear before I start an interaction with someone where I feel like there is something that I'd like them to see. I have made it a practice to ask for permission before I speak. I do not ask you to do the same, but I have come to see this unasked advice as a form of arrogance. "What makes me think that I know better?" I'll ask myself. As my mentor, Cees de Bruin, often said, "Your intentions do not change the outcome of your actions." Even when we think we're doing good, we often screw things up.

How do we feel the intention behind our words? It starts with that word "feel." We must feel what is compelling us to speak. I ask myself, "Why am I speaking now?" More often than not, I'm simply reacting to something triggered by what the other has said. And I find that I am compelled to speak more when the thing I see in another person is something I have not yet made peace with in myself.

The reason for this is quite clear. Being around people who mirror back to us the things we haven't healed in ourselves can be exhausting. Now that it's right in front of our face, we are driven to fix it in the other—if not for them, then for our own peace of mind. As this process often goes unnoticed, it's problematic, because although we believe our intentions to heal the other are good, our motivation is something totally different: to calm the tension in our own system. Rather than trying to help the other, we're actually being quite selfish. A typical reaction we hear when people feel their advice is not being taken is, "I'm only trying to help."

So, back to our original question: How do I allow my intentions to support my interactions? After I've asked myself, "Why am I speaking?" there is a split second where an answer pops up, and then my literal mind takes over. Think of a horror movie or prank internet video where the screen switches for a split second to a scary face and then flips back to the same scene. The answer to that question is never in my head. It's always somewhere deeper—somewhere that's not easy to look.

When I get that flash, I know there is something more to what I'm about to say. Something in the other's words is touching me in such a way that I feel compelled to speak.

Then I ask myself the next question: "What's the hardest thing to admit?" The answer to this question always brings me closer to my own emotions. I do not need to speak the answer out loud. That often confuses people. I simply feel what I'm having a hard time acknowledging or accepting.

The answer to this question gives me two things. First is calm. It helps me center myself and, like a strings musician, tune my instrument before speaking. And secondly, it helps me stay in touch with the things that may bleed into my intentions.

As I said, if I'm about to speak in order to help another person, I always ask for permission. And if I feel judgment toward this person, I share that so it's transparent: "I must admit that I have been judging you" or, "Before I say anything, I have to acknowledge that I don't feel impartial." I show my intentions clearly, which makes it hard for the other to dismiss what I have to say. The one thing a person might say is, "You are totally missing the point, but at least you're open about it."

The most important lesson from this chapter is this: It is not our job to fix anyone. If we feel that need and we speak, then there is something that we have not made peace with in ourselves. To the degree that we are unable to make peace with that thing, we will try to help others and find that many are not receptive to it. We will often get rejected and/or feel resentful. That is the plight of the blind healer.

The way to turn this around is to realize that whatever we think is immaterial. Our thoughts and judgments of others are simply ideas that we've attached to. But those thoughts are only relevant if the other finds them valuable. I may know the secret to solving all the world's problems, but if everyone I tell is running away from me, how does it help anyone?

When interacting with another, always trust that your intentions are good. There is nothing to judge in yourself. Then realize that just because your intentions are good does not mean that you need to speak. In fact, one of the greatest gifts in communications is listening. The more we understand ourselves, the more we see that people want to feel heard. And the ability to listen is always more important than whatever we have to say.

✳ ✳ ✳

Lesson: Before speaking, check your intentions.

Exercise 15: Pick Your Poison

This chapter has been all about self-awareness. How do we make sure that when we speak, we are not falling into the trap of thinking that we know better and trying to fix the other?

For that, we need to be able to ask ourselves, "Why am I speaking now?" There is always an easy answer: maybe, "Because it was my turn" or, "Because I felt like it." Although both of those answers might be true, this Pick Your Poison exercise is asking you to look a bit deeper.

For each situation, pick which sentence most closely matches why you want to speak.

Situation ❶

A dear friend has gotten into the same problem again and again. You have watched them explain why this time it's going to be different, and you're not buying it.

You speak because:

Ⓐ You are desperate to help them not make the same mistake.

Ⓑ You are frustrated that they continue to make the same mistake.

Ⓒ You have a great idea if they'd only listen.

Ⓓ You've been making the same mistake, and you'd like for at least one of you to solve it.

Situation ❷

Your closest family member is getting into some trouble at work. You know deep in your heart that if things don't change, they're going to lose their job.

You speak because:

- Ⓐ They are unaware, and you know they need your guidance.
- Ⓑ You are scared for them.
- Ⓒ You are the oldest child, and you feel like it is your role.
- Ⓓ You know if they lose their job, you'll be asked for money.

As you may have guessed, there is no winning this game, ergo the name. This game was created to amplify the challenges that we face when we are confronted with people in our lives who make decisions that we see are not serving them. It can be a real challenge not to jump in and help, but it is important to slow down and check in with yourself.

LISTEN TO THE CHAPTER

CHAPTER 16

Influence Versus Manipulation

It's hard to write a chapter on intention without following it up with the distinction between influence and manipulation. I know that word semantics can be challenging to pay attention to, so I'll keep it short; maybe imagining that I am singing this to you in a clown voice will help.

These are more than just words. Think of the distinction as a knob that when turned the wrong way will electrocute you. Why is this so important? If we want someone to do something, we have choices about how to influence them to do it. And if you think back to some recent chapters, the answer may already be forming in your head.

For years, I juggled with questions like, "If someone gets you to do something you may not have otherwise done and there are negative consequences, can we say that it was manipulation?" The person felt as if they were doing a good thing, but in the end, the results were not positive.

Take, for example, a friend, Will, who has made a lot of money on the stock market. He was so excited about his newfound wealth that he convinced another friend of mine, Carlos, to sell everything that he owned and join him in Thailand, living off the gains on the stock market. He arrived to Thailand in 2008, on the very day of one of the worst losses in the history of the stock market. He lost most of his money and was forced to return home and start over again. In the end, the friend possibly felt manipulated. If the stocks had gone up, thought, he might have felt grateful. How do we decide whether he was manipulated?

When I began working as a coach and mentor, I needed to know when I was overstepping my boundaries and potentially getting people to do things they might suffer from later. The first major conclusion I came to: through my mere existence, I influence others. It can't be controlled. If I sit silently in a meeting with two others, I influence the dynamic with my silence—possibly even significantly. There is no avoiding influencing people around us. So how do we monitor ourselves? If we think we have a great idea to share with someone, how do we bring it forward responsibly?

To that end, I often use the word we spoke of in Chapter 12, "agency." This word is associated with the reliance a person has on me to navigate their life. The more they rely on me, the more they lose agency over themselves. The less they rely on me, the more they maintain their agency. If I believe I know something the other does not, I may begin to exert influence over them. It's subtle—a comment here, a story there: "I wouldn't do it that way," "You need to change your approach," or a quick remark: "Interesting." All this is said to "help" the other person see or understand something. I have begun influencing them, possibly without them knowing it.

When does this influence then become manipulation? To answer this question, we must go back to the previous chapter on intentions. If we mean well but lead someone in a direction that proves abysmal, then that's exerting an influence that happens to have negative consequences. Although it may prove painful for all parties, it does not reach the level of manipulation. If, however, we lead someone in a direction that we know will be detrimental to them, that is manipulation under my definition.

The bigger question for me is how to steer clear of even moving slightly in the direction of manipulation. For that we again return to agency. I have found this to be a far better lens with which to view my interactions with others.

If I exert enough influence on a person, they very well may let go of their agency and base their decisions on my experience, not their own. Regardless, whether the decision serves them or not, it's still their decision to make.

To better understand this, I turn to a story from an executive coach that I once had contact with. He was incredibly charismatic and certain of himself. He spoke in superlatives and was quick to tell you how much he was making and all the ways in which you were not living to your fullest potential. He created an emotional gap in those whom he spoke with so that he could then fill it with a course of his own.

Of course, there was no ill intent, but as we already know, that does not mean that there weren't negative consequences. Many of his students began to lose agency over their decision-making, which eventually led several to seek guidance to regain their confidence. As you might imagine, the coach blamed the students without taking any responsibility for the damage caused. The commonality of the experience of those who lost themselves was resounding: "How could I have allowed myself to be so misled?"

This is why I spend a lot of time working through my own beliefs before interacting with others. When we do not see our need to help and caretake, we push people unknowingly—and there are real consequences. In a conscious relationship, our job is to support others in *their* journey, not to arrogantly suppose that we know what's best for them.

Of course, I recognize that there are ages and situations where a person is unable to have complete agency in their lives. Teenagers and drug addicts come to mind. But in instances where the likelihood of self-harm is low, other people's journeys are theirs to make in the way and at the speed they choose.

It can be incredibly difficult to surrender to another person's journey, especially when we feel they are making decisions and exhibiting behavior that does not serve them. I make the decision to either accept people as they are or separate myself from them without blame. That's how we ensure that our influence does not push people who may eventually feel as if they were manipulated.

It's not always an easy way to live. We see so many things in others that we believe need to be addressed to improve their lives. But it's not our responsibility. And in the end, when we push too hard, the people we're trying to support will often resent us for it. We must always remember that another's life is theirs to lead, not ours.

※ ※ ※

Lesson: Never assume you are helping someone.

Exercise 16: Four Doors

This chapter pointed out an important lesson when it comes to helping others: we must realize that our help can lead to unforeseen consequences. Namely, people can lose trust in themselves and their ability to make decisions for themselves. To get a better understanding of how to heighten your consciousness around this subject, I offer the Four Doors exercise. Are you able to walk through all of the four doors?

Situation

You feel compelled to help or offer advice to a friend or family member.

Door 1: Am I willing to accept that this may be the perfect thing for them at this stage in their life?

Door 2: Am I willing to accept that whatever they choose to do is fine?

Door 3: Am I willing to accept that it's their decision to make and not mine?

Door 4: Am I willing to accept that it's not easy for me to surrender to the journey of another?

If you answered yes to the four questions, then you have passed through the four doors. When we are unable or unwilling to surrender to the journey of another, it bleeds into our interactions. In the best-case scenario, we help the other change their life. In the worst, we undermine their confidence going forward. It's not easy. We see issues and feel it's essential that we speak up, and often it is. But we cannot be blind to our own intentions.

CHAPTER 17

The Why Before the What

We can unknowingly create situations that cause others to feel disconnected even before we begin an interaction. It would not be dissimilar to serving dinner without eating utensils and looking down at your food in anticipation.

To avoid creating this tension, I set a context for myself and those around me before undertaking anything important. Setting context is essential if we want people to take a journey with us. If we fail to do this, people often lose interest and separate. This concept is particularly important in groups, where it's easier for people to hide.

All of this may seem obvious, but people often assume that everyone knows why we are here. "Isn't it obvious?" they think and jump right over it. When we create a context, we not only set an outline of what to expect but also get the buy-in. We are sharing a narrative to get people to connect to us and what we are trying to achieve.

A good context has three important elements:

1 How did we get here?

2 Where are we going now?

3 What is our intended outcome?

Good context setting is very much tied to good storytelling. The picture created in peoples' minds helps them sense the actions that will follow. Of course, this comes easier to some, but it's a skill that can be learned. I often had long discussions with Rani where I'd jump into a thought without giving her a context for it.

I've always wanted to live on or close to a farm. We would talk about this for hours, and it usually led nowhere.

"Andy, I was raised on a farm in Indonesia. The last thing I want to do is end up back on one." Then it hit me that I had never shared with her the context for how I saw our future together—why I was discussing the topic to begin with.

"Babe, the cold and rainy Amsterdam winters are really tough on me. This is not going to work long-term for me. It's depressing. I'd love to start looking for something warmer in the winter. I always feel more at home in the countryside, so I'd love to hear how you see it. Whatever we do, I would like to be thinking on a two- to three-year time horizon, as I don't know how much longer I can manage the winters."

Two years later, we purchased a farm in Spain, where I am currently sitting next to the fire and writing this book (with a smug smile on my face).

The importance of context can be underestimated because it takes time away from the "discussion time." But for me, it's the most important thing to do at the start of anything meaningful. It's what makes people decide to either pay attention or not. It's where we begin to get the buy-in or lose people before even starting.

When creating a context, it's exceptionally helpful to personalize it. As far as we make it about ourselves, people will see and understand us and why this topic is important. This goes back to many of the lessons in previous chapters. The more a context is emotionally removed from us (i.e., told without showing any vulnerability), the easier it is for people to make assumptions about our intent and purpose.

Consider this example in business:

Question 1: How did we get here?
Non-personalized: "Hello, group. The leadership has been

discussing strategy, and we decided to arrange a meeting to discuss it with you."

Personalized: "Hello, group. After years of being asked what our strategy is and never feeling comfortable answering the question, this project was created."

In the first example, we see a remote explanation for what is to come. In the latter, we begin to identify with the leader and her intentions.

If we take another step:

Question 2: Where are we going?

Non-personalized: "So we will be spending the next hours discussing this."

Personalized: "So as part of the process, we will be spending the next hours together so that we can better understand your experiences and how those will shape our strategy going forward."

Again, we see the difference it makes when the leader tells participants what will happen versus inviting them to participate in the process.

And finally, we have the desired outcome, or intention:

Question 3: What is our intended outcome?

Non-personalized: "In the end, I hope we can both understand this a bit better."

Personalized: "In the end, I hope that you see how your experience is at the heart of our strategy and that we, as a team, are excited and confident executing on it."

Here we see the distinction between remaining remote and sharing the end as an experience that one can imagine.

When we share something as a state that people can experience, it becomes clearer and provides guidance. It's like the well-known example of the cut lemon. Imagine yourself biting into it, and feel your mouth begin to salivate. The more visceral the experience, the more people will connect to us and our desired outcome. It's the difference between saying, "I'd like you to understand" and, "By the end of this meeting, I want you to feel comfortable sharing this strategy with a friend so they understand it in less than a minute." Talking in experiences helps people understand our state of mind, which opens up a deeper sense of knowing.

Also, if the starting context is strong, trust is established with the listener. A person feels as if they are being taken care of and there is someone taking responsibility for the process forward. When the starting context is weak, the opposite occurs. People turn off and lose confidence in our message.

Until now, I have spoken about the use of context primarily in business, but it is no different in personal relationships. If we are about to begin a challenging talk with our partner, there are many ways to go about it, and the one we choose will set the stage for what follows.

"You aren't listening to me."

"Honey, I see that over the last weeks when I say something, you'll often interrupt me in the middle [observation]. I'd like to share something that's hard for me [vulnerability]. I know there is something that you'd like to say, but would you be willing to hear me out first?"

In these two examples, we see how the context is set. Of course, this does not guarantee a positive outcome, but it does set the stage for what is to come.

An easy place to see how lack of context impacts us is with email. How many times have you received an email from someone asking you to meet, with no context provided for the meeting? As the receiver, you are left wondering the reason: "Is there a problem? Do I need to prepare? Do I need to be worried?"

When we fail to set clear context, a lot of space is created for others to fill it in with a story. As I once told a leader I was coaching, "If you let them interpret, it will almost never be in your favor." A simple context can make a profound difference in conversations.

✳ ✳ ✳

Lesson: Set a clear context before starting important conversations.

Exercise 17: Sort It Out

In this exercise, you are asked to sort the group of three sentences into the correct order following the steps discussed earlier in this chapter.

❶ *How did we get here?*
❷ *Where are we going now?*
❸ *What is our intended outcome?*

Order ❶ ❷ ❸	Statement
	"I'd love to talk about how we can get things flowing between us again."
	"I've been struggling, and I'd like to discuss our relationship."
	"I feel like there are things we can discuss to improve our relations."

Order ① ② ③	Statement
	"This meeting will give us a chance to begin planning the transition."
	"I hope that by the end everyone will feel better about where we are heading."
	"Due to staff changes, we are here to discuss some important changes."

Order ① ② ③	Statement
	"If you are free for lunch tomorrow, I would love to discuss what you plan to do in the future."
	"I saw what you published online today, and I was hoping to talk with you."
	"It would be great to see if there is a chance that we could find some overlaps in our activities."

RECAP

In making a connection with others, the little things matter. Taking the time to give people a sense of understanding and shared purpose is critical to getting the buy-in early and setting ourselves up for a meaningful connection. Setting the context for what is to come is a great way to begin anything where we want people to join us on a journey.

CHAPTER RECAP VIDEO

CHAPTER 18

Priming Mind

Priming occurs in the time before the start of, during, and even after an interaction, when one's mind is preparing or supporting an experience.

Have you ever wondered why transformational seminars are held at beautiful retreat centers with unobstructed views? The simple answer might be, "Because they are beautiful." But there is a whole lot more to it.

Our brains create associations that are reinforced by our environment. Some environments reinforce negative or positive experiences. A room with no windows gives people a sense of confinement. Add a window overlooking the ocean to that one room, and the feeling completely shifts. Many studies have explained this phenomenon, but instead of going into those, I would ask you to go back into your own experience. How do you feel when you look out the window at a beautiful landscape versus at a wall?

Imagine arranging a team-building exercise and holding it in the same environment where the team has been struggling. Many disappointments have been shared in that room, and it is hard to separate from those feelings, which makes it even harder to muster up inspiration. Our mind may want to believe we can make it work, but our body holds on to the past.

This is why I spend a lot of time priming before beginning a training or an important interaction. I like to create a state of mind in participants. This can be done in a variety of ways: emails, pictures, little gifts that percolate in people's minds before they arrive. This creates a sense of excitement for what is to come and also gets people ready to participate before arriving to the event.

One study stands out for me regarding how much priming impacts performance. A group of Asian American women were asked to perform a math task, but before doing so, the group was primed to a stereotype. One of the stereotypes was "Asians are good at math," while the other was, "Women are not good at math." A third group was not primed at all. The study found that when the women were primed with an Asian identity, they performed the best, while those primed with a female identity performed the worst. It shows how when we identify with something, we also identify with the stereotypes that accompany that identity.

Priming has an amazing influence on people. I recently had a client ask me for advice. One of her team members had made a repeated mistake. She wanted to send him an email saying, "I'd like to talk next week." She had me read the email and asked me what I thought.

After we discussed a bit, I asked, "Is he aware that you are unhappy?"

She responded, "I don't think so."

"Would you like him to feel uncomfortable before you speak?"

"Yes," she said.

I suggested she change the email to, "I was unhappy to see what occurred. I'd like to arrange a talk next week to discuss."

Although it's subtle, she is priming the team member for what is to come. In the period between his reading the email and the actual meeting, he will be reflecting, and much of the work will be done by the time the talk occurs. This is priming for that meeting.

Although this topic may not be the most essential, it is important to note and is often missed—especially when creating events. Before someone joins you at an event or meeting, their mind is tangled in the day-to-day routine of work. It takes at least a half day to get people out of that mental state. Priming can help accelerate this process. I've seen this best done by controlling the environment—in addition to using communication leading up to the event.

A friend of mine is a relationship therapist. She shared with me that one of the biggest challenges she has when supporting couples is issues around sex. Specifically, how her clients communicate about it. She told me, "It's not something you want to discuss right before or during. It kills the moment. So I always suggest that my clients read a romance novel together and share what they liked about it. It gives space for each to share without the pressure or overanalysis, which kills the spontaneity and experimentation of the moment." In other words, a bit of priming beforehand can make a huge difference in our intimate lives.

I spend a lot of time thinking about priming in my own life when I work with groups. I am always asking myself, "How am I, through my words and actions, not giving people clear expectations of what I am looking to achieve?"

When I was a manager, I really wanted to be liked. I would do my best to make everything feel as if things were okay, even when they were not. The consequence of this behavior was that I primed the people around me to feel complacent. This, of course, led me to feel more stressed.

Because I was so focused on their comfort, I undermined my ability to manage. This changed when I saw that I did not need to be liked—not that I needed to be disliked, but I did not need to go out of my way to be liked. I learned how to better prime people for interactions. I no longer avoided mentioning the elephant in the room before meetings. In fact, I would welcome it and show that it was not necessarily a problem but certainly needed to be addressed.

I had been priming the people around me to not take their actions seriously. Why would they? Andy was not going to hold them accountable. When this changed, the people around me began taking more personal responsibility because I primed them to see what was expected. I did this by implementing more and more processes that set clearer expectations. Going back to the chapter on setting context, I also shared what was changing and why: "I see that I have not always been a good manager because I have not given you an understanding of what was expected. I can imagine that it was not always easy to know what to focus on and how that would be measured, so I apologize for not being clearer sooner. From now on, I plan to implement a system that helps us all work better. I look forward to your support in getting there."

In the above, I was transitioning to holding others and myself more accountable. In time, it worked. As you very well know, very little changes after a single mention. It often takes weeks, months, sometimes years to shift a company culture. By priming people's minds, we support them to be better prepared for what is to come.

✳ ✳ ✳

Lesson: Prime before for deeper connection.

Exercise 18: Prime Choice

In this chapter, we discussed how to make sure that people come into and leave your events, meetings, and important moments engaged and ready to participate. This can be done with grand gestures, like gifts, or the use of words like "important" or "special." In this exercise, Prime Choice, you will be given a few scenarios. Choose the action that primes well for the activity to follow.

You are going into a meeting, and you'd like your boss to consider a pay raise.

- (A) You share that you would like to discuss your salary before the meeting.
- (B) You ask your boss how long it normally takes to get a pay rise.
- (C) You check in with the HR department and ask for the policy regarding pay raises.
- (D) You send a short email detailing your pay increases over the last five years before the meeting.
- (E) All of the above.

You are meeting a friend, and you'd like for them to be there on time.

- (A) You send them a message the day before and ask them to contact you if they are going to be late.
- (B) You send them a text twenty minutes before you meet and ask them where they are.
- (C) You choose a location that you know is easy for them to get to and let them know the reason you chose that location.

Ⓓ You share that it's important for you that they are on time because you will need to leave after an hour.

Ⓔ All of the above.

You are doing a presentation, and you'd like people to come with questions.

Ⓐ You send out your presentation ahead and tell people that there is something in the slides that they should have a look at before coming.

Ⓑ You share with all the attendees that you'd like for everyone to have at least one question ready.

Ⓒ You purchase a secret gift and tell the attendees that the best question wins the prize.

Ⓓ You send out three questions that have already been asked so that people see that others have already come up with questions.

Ⓔ All of the above.

You are going to be spending the weekend with a friend, and you want there to be a sense of excitement.

Ⓐ You send a countdown each day.

Ⓑ You send them a list of the activities that you can do during the weekend.

Ⓒ You tell them that you have a special surprise for them.

Ⓓ You send them pictures of the location with short messages.

Ⓔ All of the above.

As you may have guessed, the correct answer to all of the questions is "e) All of the above." Thinking about the mindset is really important when planning important events, meetings, and special interactions. Priming is like building the set of a play. If we build the set well, all of the actors will have an easier time falling into character. In priming, we want our efforts to have the maximum impact.

Think about the room with the blank walls or a window overlooking the sea. Which would you rather spend the day in? What happens to your mind in either location? How does this impact your nervous system? That is the power of priming.

CHAPTER 19

Letting Go to Get There

Although I don't identify with any specific religious or spiritual tradition, I resonate with the Buddhist teaching of nonattachment in my approach to communication. The Buddha taught that when we are attached to a desire for something, we suffer. We can be attached to people, things, situations, or simply ideas.

Attachment bleeds into all our communications and can alienate others. I've found that when I want something, people feel it. If I try to steer the direction of a conversation to get my desired outcome, people know and often resist it. In short, as I've alluded to before, people resist me to the degree that I push them. Or as Newton's third law states, every action will have an opposite and equal reaction.

When we attach to an outcome, our words and actions align to get it. We emit an energy we are not aware of. Think of how magnets are attracted to their opposites. If two people are equally attached to the same outcome, it's like attaching a positive and negative magnet. They pop together instantly. On the other hand, if outcomes are at odds, it's like trying to attach magnets with the same charge. They immediately repel one another.

Another of life's paradoxes is that we need to have an outcome in mind to know where we want to end up. At the same time, attaching to that outcome makes it harder to get there. I can hear some readers protesting, "Andy, you cannot live without focusing on outcome. How else would we get anywhere?" I would certainly agree. I'm only saying that by focusing on an outcome, we are likely to unknowingly alienate others.

Reflect on a situation where you wanted something and someone in your life either did not support your goal or actively resisted it. You felt frustrated. You may have had thoughts like, "If only he/she did what I wanted, life would be so much easier." Now think of how you interact with that person under the impetus of this energy. Can you feel yourself pushing? Even if you try to hide it, it's there. Everything in your body is pushing you in a direction to solve or get to an outcome.

Here's where I tell you to stop doing that. What's the likelihood that's going to work? As a concept, not going after an outcome may be easy to understand. But embodying it is something different. How does one want something and at the same time let go of that outcome?

When I began my self-realization journey, I quit my job, sold everything that I owned, and found my mentor, Cees. I was determined to help all of my friends experience his work. We offered free classes and workshops. We published articles, and I spoke to just about everyone I met about his work and what I perceived as the opportunity.

The outcome I was determined to achieve was changing the world. "If we got everyone to experience this, what an impact that would have on the world," I told myself. You probably do not need to hear more of the story to realize how this energy was met. Several people in my environment simply separated themselves for fear of hearing me speak about it. In my determination to achieve, I lost sight of my contact with others.

It is in balancing these two forces, outcome orientation and connection, that we can communicate and connect with others more effectively. The trick that I've found is not to let go of the outcome but rather to not let it get in the way, like Lady Justice holding up the scale and feeling the weight of both sides balancing each other out.

I've learned how to balance this in two ways. The first is owning the outcome. I allow myself to feel it, to see that I truly want the outcome, without pretending otherwise or feeling guilt or shame for wanting it. It's typical for people to want something but deny it: "I don't really care how it turns out." This lack of honesty and ownership simply denies our desires; it doesn't get rid of them.

In my desperation to share what I'd learned from Cees, I was unable to fully own the vision I was carrying, which created suspicion around my intentions. I was trying to convince my friends and family to join without fully embodying what I was asking. If I had felt comfortable saying, "I am trying to change the world," many would have judged that desire as unrealistic, but at least they would have seen and understood me and my intentions.

So far in this chapter I've focused on outcomes in terms of the things we want, but the same is true for the things we don't want. I've written extensively on how our life changes if we suppress our true feelings in my book *The Wounded Healer*. When we "own" our suffering, our relationship with it shifts. We are less driven by our desire to avoid it. We have more space to think and act. New opportunities are made possible. Fully owning our desires and fears gives us the space to breathe.

The other side of the scale is embracing that it's okay if the outcome does not occur. You heard that correctly. First we fully embrace that we desperately want it; then we make total peace with the fact that it may never happen.

You may be thinking, "If you make peace with the fact that it may never happen, you'll lack the determination to fight to get it." I will not argue this point, but I would like to give more context to understand why accepting that the outcome may not be achieved is so important.

For that, I present the life of my father as example. At a young age, he was told that he was not smart and would not amount to much. His mother especially would nag him. As he grew up, he desperately wanted to prove his intelligence. When I was a child, he would tell people he was a CPA, not just an accountant, because achieving the title of CPA meant that he had passed an exhaustive accounting exam.

To prove himself, my father bought expensive cars and jewelry. He worked harder and harder to make more money to show off his achievements. He spent so much of his time fighting to achieve an outcome that he did not prioritize anything else in his life. He never watched me compete in a sporting event. He never went to a parent meeting or even asked me how I was doing.

As I write this, I am cautious not to judge my father nor turn myself into a victim. I share this story to say that my father never gave himself a chance to do anything else. He was so focused on the outcome that he neglected to consider the possible implications for the world around him.

In the years before his death, he shared this regret with me. As far as I was concerned, there was nothing for him to feel shame around, nor did I add to his suffering by sharing my own pain. The point of all of this can be reduced back to where we started. If we make peace with the fact that we may never achieve the thing we most desire, we can free ourselves. In the case of my father, he was not able to make peace with the thought, "I will never amount to anything," so that thought defined a great deal of his existence. If he had been able to find balance, his life might have looked far different.

In achieving this balance, a very distinct state emerges. I like to call this the state of emergence: we are not forcing things to come into being, and at the same time, we are not pushing them away. We're inviting without force.

Here is exactly where we introduce the most important tool in our arsenal of creating meaningful connection: questions. We can only ask questions that bring us close to one another when we have first made peace with our own desires. Otherwise, it's almost impossible to ask questions that do not guide the discussion or push for an outcome. A perfect example of this is seen in management. "Are you going to get it done on time?" "Do you have it under control?"

These questions are fine, and sometimes necessary. But they often don't get to "what's hidden"—the things lying beneath the surface that give us a much more realistic picture of what's happening.

By asking questions that push for an outcome, we may get blindsided by things we missed by not asking better questions. Questions like, "What might get in the way of this project getting completed on time?" "What is causing you anxiety at the moment?" "What's your biggest challenge at the moment?"

Through these questions, we express a desire to understand and support. By answering these questions, the individual is supported in anticipating challenges, and we have a better understanding of what is going on behind the scenes. Interestingly, the consequence of asking such questions is that the project is more likely to finish on time, even though the questions were not focused on the outcome.

When we heighten our consciousness around our desired outcome and let go emotionally, it's easier to ask better questions. Better questions give people a chance to reflect without being pushed, which leads to greater vulnerability and a higher likelihood that they will ask for assistance. In this environment, we find we are more likely to reach our goals, without making achieving them the focus of all our efforts.

For this book to manifest, I had to follow my own understanding. When I started, I had just finished my second book, *The Wounded Healer*. I felt like there was another one ready to come out of me. As with all of my books, I did not know what it was going to be ahead of time, but I knew that it needed to find its way into the world.

Instead of letting the process unfold as I had in the first two books, I began to manage it. I set aside two months over the Christmas holidays to write. The holidays came, and I sat in bed with no inspiration. Instead of doing what I normally do, laughing and surrendering to the moment, I tried to write.

As you might expect, it was an uphill battle. Each sentence felt like a struggle, as I was pushing against my feelings. I finally gave in and surrendered, acknowledging that this was not the time. I left the book for six months, not knowing if I would ever pick it up again.

For some reason that I cannot explain, I once again felt inspired and began writing. I surrendered to the feeling that it might not happen, and it came back to me with all the excitement I began with.

What I saw was that letting go of the idea that this book had to be created made it a connective and emotionally rewarding journey. As I write, I am very aware that this is my particular way of working. Many people need structure and outside pressure to get things done. There are indeed times that I need the same just to get motivated. And yet, when I surrender to the process and allow myself to be free and write from that place, the words flow from me.

✳ ✳ ✳

Lesson: Attaching to an outcome pushes people and opportunities away.

Exercise 19: Lady Justice

This chapter was all about simultaneously embracing both the focus on outcomes and surrendering to reality. In order to create this as an experience, we are going to do the Lady Justice exercise. The statements below will help you to find this balance. Complete the sentences by writing your answers in the specified sections.

Embrace:

I really, really want . . .

_____

_____

_____

I am totally focused on making [previous answer] a reality.

Surrender:

I am at peace with the fact that [answer] may never happen.

_____

_____

_____

I have nothing to prove. I am complete with and without [answer].

In this section, we practiced how to find balance in our lives. We do this so that we can remain present. If we completely dedicate ourselves to achieving our goals and at the same time make peace with the chance that they may never happen, we come back to the here and now. This does not mean that we give up on our goals; rather, we do not let our goals blind us to the way we get there.

SECTION V

Advanced Skills for Deepening Connection

CHAPTER 20

Listening Without Prejudice

As you have already gathered by now, one of my favorite pastimes is pointing out paradoxes. And listening is one of the ones I enjoy most. In silence we can teach more than through words.

One of the biggest challenges to teaching people how to communicate is getting them to shut up. Unfortunately, many people listen so they can speak. Put another way, they hold on to their thought until the other is finished speaking. Which means they were never really listening to begin with. A good listener will often get lost in another person's words. Rather than holding on to their own thoughts, they allow what is active in the moment to define the interaction.

In meetings, we may notice the one quiet person in the room. They do not say much, but they often have the best grasp of what is going on around them. On the few occasions they do speak, it's filled with an insight that makes us wonder, "If they see that so clearly, what else do they see?"

In one such meeting, I was with a group of people who were discussing the behavior of a client. The meeting went around and around in circles until someone eventually asked the quietest person in the group what she thought. The answer was simple, but it cut so deep that everyone's focus shifted: "Instead of asking how to get into the meeting, why not ask why they don't trust us enough to invite us there?"

There are certainly different ways to listen. But I want to reinforce that to start, we need to be quiet. I'm stating the obvious, but many people believe that listening is about talking, about saying what they think until another person adopts the same ideas. This is not the case. Once we are quiet, there is space. Think of a room filled with a limited amount of oxygen. If we are speaking and taking up all the oxygen, we're don't leave a lot of air for anyone else.

I once had lunch with a lawyer who spent the entire lunch speaking. It was quite exhausting for me because listening takes concentration. At one point in the middle of his ramblings, he said, "I am a great listener."

I laughed and said, "How does that work, since you are often talking?"

We were friends, so he laughed good-naturedly and said, "No, I really am a good listener." Then he proceeded to keep talking.

We avoid quiet because most of us find it uncomfortable. We may not have the peace within ourselves to withstand that moment of emptiness. Instead of letting the quiet create space, we fill it with noise. The avoidance of silence can go quite far.

One study placed participants alone in a room with nothing but a machine that allowed them to shock themselves. They were asked to sit in that room alone and in silence for fifteen minutes. Shockingly (pun intended), sitting silently was so hard for them that 67 percent of men and 25 percent of women chose to shock themselves rather than sit with their thoughts.[3]

In 2020, I spent every weekday for an entire year doing a talk show called *A Wonderful Chaos*. At the start of one of the shows, my partner and I agreed not to speak unless we had something essential to say. We ended up spending an hour—on a live broadcast—looking at the camera in silence. It was unplanned and taught us both an important lesson. So many of the things we say are inessential. We often speak because it's easy to speak, not because it's important. We are filling the air with noise.

When I was in my thirties, I was terrified of silence. It brought me back to my childhood fear of death. I would compensate for this fear by calling person after person and booking my calendar solid with appointments. Anything to be busy. It got so bad that my boss called me into his office to ask me to bring my telephone bill to under $1,000 a month. I was filling my time with people to avoid my own loneliness. And since I was unable to connect to quiet, I spent a lot of that time talking.

How this shows up in life is in what I call "transactional communications." You say what you have to say, and I'll say what I have to say. Then repeat. We were raised with this way of communication. In fact, it's a big part of our education. We are educated to argue our point. To make ourselves understood. There are even debate classes that teach us how to develop arguments for one side or another.

The benefit of these classes is that they teach one to argue both sides equally well. The downside is that the concept is based on arguing. We learn at an early age that making a point is important— that it's imperative to be right, to have an opinion. We see people who hold strong ideas as strong and praise them publicly, even electing them into public office. From an early age, listening is rarely nourished or deemed valuable as a trait or skill.

It's only when we want things from others that we begin to see how not listening has consequences. People want to be heard. Engaging with someone without listening is setting ourselves up for failure. It's logical. We are asking another to take interest in our desires while not doing the same in return.

"You are not listening to me," she says as she raises her voice.

"No, *you're* not listening to *me*," he responds with the same intensity.

Neither side realizes that at that very moment, they are not giving the other person the very thing they are asking for themselves.

Through listening, we give others a reason to care about what we have to say. We make the other person feel heard. Please notice the phrasing here. The other needs to "feel heard." The hard truth is that *we* do not decide if another person feels heard. They do.

I can usually tell if another person feels heard by the way they interact with me. They are relaxed. They share more. They show a level of trust. They are vulnerable.

If we hear ourselves thinking about what we are about to say while another person is speaking, then we are probably not listening. As people speak, our mind gets flooded with thoughts, and it is not easy to settle them in the middle of an interaction. When we attach to one of those thoughts and get drawn away from the other person, we are no longer paying attention. We miss the important parts. We don't clue in to the emotional moments.

The worst part is that other people notice this. We've all had the experience of telling someone something important only to realize they aren't listening. It never feels good. Of course, we rarely, if ever, tell the other person we know they were not listening. Instead, we walk away hurt; meanwhile, the other person thinks they got away with something.

I have been known to carry a pen and piece of paper around with me to write things down as they come up in conversations. This allows me to stay present and continue listening while also being able to come back to things I want to discuss. Just because I'm listening doesn't mean that I'm not also reacting to what is being said.

Being a good listener compensates for just about any other communication skill you may be lacking. As most great leaders will say openly, I can teach you a skill. What I can't teach you is the predisposition needed to be successful in the job.

As I mentioned earlier, I have been given many opportunities for which I was completely unqualified, in large part due to how well I listened. And it's important to note that I was always honest about my qualifications. I never lied about my background or experience.

I worked once with a client, a human resources director for a large manufacturing company, who was tired of her job and looking for a change. She told me, "Andy, I'm sick of this job. I've been working in HR for over twenty years, and I can't take it anymore."

"What would you like to do?" I asked.

She said, "It may sound strange, but I want to do marketing."

I thought for a moment, and instead of saying something like "But you don't have any marketing experience," I said, "Well, why don't you find a few open positions and interview for them."

A bit surprised, she agreed. A week later, she showed me an ad for a marketing position with one of the largest local fashion retailers. She said, "This looks interesting, but there is no way I'd get such a position."

"Go ahead and apply," I urged.

And she did. After submitting her application, she asked me, "But what do I tell them in the interview? I have no formal marketing experience."

I replied, "In the interview, just ask them a few questions. Start with, 'What are the qualities you are looking for in this candidate?' Let them speak. Then ask, 'And what else?' Let them speak some more.

"As they are speaking, note anything you cannot do, and tell them when they are finished. Say, 'From what I've heard, I'd be comfortable doing everything you mentioned, except for [what you noticed]. And I'm confident I can get up to speed in that area.'

"And then your final question to ask your interviewer is 'What would you like to know about me to see that I'm the right candidate for this role?'

"When they bring up your lack of marketing experience, share how everything you've done in HR has related to marketing."

My client went through the interview and called me afterward. "We were like old friends," she said. "At the end, I think we were both a bit confused as to why we were so comfortable with each other." Two weeks later, she was offered the job. This is what listening makes possible. It's not the golden bullet for everything, but it puts people way ahead in the line.

Lesson: Listening well begins with silence.

Exercise 20: Hold Your Tongue

For this exercise, you will need to let go of your immediate desire to speak. You will feel yourself let go of the need to be heard or defend. To do this exercise, you need a bit of imagination. There are four situations below. Fully place yourself in each of these situations and see how you react. Stay silent for thirty seconds after reading each situation. Make notes afterwards, if it's helpful.

Your partner yells, "Why aren't you listening to me!"

 (Take thirty-second pause.)

Your boss tells you, "You have got to improve your communication skills."

 (Take thirty-second pause.)

One of your parents tells you, "You are not being a good son/daughter."

 (Take thirty-second pause.)

A friend tells you, "You never defend me in public."

 (Take thirty-second pause.)

It is not easy to remain silent, especially when we feel under attack. Our ability to give space for a dialogue to emerge from silence is an important part of creating connection. In the above situations, you may have felt the urge to react in either attack or retreat. In your next interactions, see what happens when you allow more silence. The results may very well surprise you.

LISTEN TO THE CHAPTER

CHAPTER 21

Ask Skillful Questions

I said that listening is largely just being quiet, which is not completely true. If we are simply quiet, then conversations lead nowhere. That's not necessarily a problem, because sometimes listening is just about letting the other person blow off steam. Think of the typical relationship when one partner complains and the other falls into problem-solving mode. It often ends in a fight. "How about you . . ." or "Why not . . ." are just a few of the statements we might hear.

Listening is about creating space with quiet. And now we add the magic ingredient: questions.

It's often said that there are no bad questions. Rest assured, there are. I've often said, "Questions tell me more about the person asking them than the person receiving them." If we listen closely to questions, we find they are often a means of passing judgment. It's so subtle that we may not even notice. "Do you think it's a good idea to do that?" actually means, "I don't think it's a good idea, and I'm not comfortable saying that directly." "Have you thought about doing it another way?" is actually, "This way is going to fail, but I don't want to alienate you." "Why don't you consider . . ." is actually, "I think you should consider . . ."

We often communicate our hidden intentions through questions. This is why the previous chapters are so important. If we are blind to our intentions when asking questions, we can very easily trigger others, not realizing we are passing judgment unconsciously. Then we say something like, "It was only a question. You don't have to get defensive."

Everything from this moment forward is shared with the caveat that we can screw it up if we don't keep our intentions in check. Enough said.

As I mentioned previously, I set an intention before all of my interactions. What I have to say is unimportant. What others understand is critical. The only way I truly know what others understand is through questions. So I almost always begin, continue, and end with those.

Some people say that whoever is asking questions is leading the conversation. But this implies some level of dominance. I'd prefer to say that we ask so we can understand and help others understand themselves better. People have a lot going on in their heads. Their thoughts are often scattered, and it's not always possible to center oneself to see through it. By supporting another person with questions, we have the potential to do just that.

Questions can serve as a guide to someone's inner confusion. Or put simply, questions help people get clarity inside of themselves. Why should we invest time in that? The answer for me is uncomplicated. If we don't, nothing tends to progress, which can get aggravating. Alternatively, being there for another person is simply nice. Or it might prevent a costly divorce. We get to choose our motives. But rest assured, if we are not connecting with the others through questions, there are consequences.

There are different types of questions and ways to ask them. The first type to understand is an opening question.

Opening Questions

An opening question is the first question we ask when beginning a meaningful dialogue. It gives us context for a conversation. As mentioned in previous chapters, it's important for people to understand the space in which we want to meet them. Without that context, it's like telling a friend, "Hey, let's meet tomorrow" without designating a location.

A dialogue can go anywhere, so we begin by setting up a direction—though, importantly, we are not pushing in that direction. An opening question is never closed to anything outside a yes or no answer like, "Can we talk about what happened yesterday," or, "Are you happy?"

Two dimensions of an opening question to consider are relevance and scope. By relevance, I mean how relevant the topic is to the other person or our relationship. By scope I mean how broad we can take the dialogue without forcing it in any specific direction.

"How are you?" is a very broad question, and its relevance depends on how the other person receives the question.

A more specific question is, "I know your mom died last year. How are you?" This comes closer to touching emotion.

Let's try another: "What's going on with your friend Sue?"

Now we make it more specific: "I know Sue broke up with her boyfriend. How is she doing?" Again, we are setting the context for a more emotional dialogue when we ask questions that touch on real things.

In the service industry, the difference would be something like this at the end of a stay at a hotel.

Broad: "How can we help you?"

More specific: "Where might you like to see improvements made in our service?"

The second formulation gives a clearer context for an answer.

Open Questions

While an opening question is used to open a dialogue, an open question can be used at any point in a conversation. An open question is, as stated, open, which means it can lead anywhere, while a closed question only allows for a yes or no answer. The general rule is that an open question begins with a "w" word: what, when, why—or how. There is an important distinction to make here because we can also start questions with a verb: "Are you going?" "Have you made a reservation?" "Can you come over tomorrow?"

Asking closed questions takes less time and energy and also confirms the things we already want to believe. "Are you going to make the deadline?" "Are you happy with your time here?" "Did you enjoy your meal?" These questions are pushing in a direction. Although not impossible, it's unlikely that people will give an authentic answer in response; rather, they will likely say no out of convenience.

Now let's look at the same three questions when they become open. "What, if anything, might stop you from meeting the deadline?" "What might we improve to make your next stay with us even better?" "How were the meals for you this evening?" By changing the questions from closed to open, we immediately increase the potential for connection and understanding.

There is an added quality to closed questions that's hard to see: Closed questions have built-in assumptions. In order to ask a closed question, we must simultaneously make a statement.

Take, for example, the sentence, "Are you happy?" Unknowingly, we have introduced happiness as something the person would need to consider in order to answer the question. They did not say anything about happiness. We have made it important. And now, through this question, we've imposed a box for the other to answer within.

An open question would be, "How are you?" In that question, we are not presuming happiness or unhappiness. In fact, the one being asked can answer in any way they deem fit, perhaps something like, "I've been spending a lot of time thinking about my mom because it's her birthday today."

We see in that example how much richer a potential answer is when it's not confined by a closed question. It's important to ask ourselves, "What assumption am I making when I'm asking a closed question? How is this influencing the other in ways that I may be unaware of? How does that create a world that only gives me a small chance of hearing what is really going on? What do my relationships look like if I primarily ask closed questions?"

"Can't you see what is going on here?" he exclaims.

"No, I can't," his friend replies.

"Are you telling me that you really don't know?"

"No, I really don't."

"Are you sure?"

With closed questions, we are confirming the bias in the question. We are imposing on another something they may or may not be interested in answering. I would go as far as saying that asking closed questions is a slight form of arrogance. Who am I to presume I know anything about what's really going on in the other?

That is not to say that closed questions don't also play an important role. We will get into that soon. However, going back to the chapter on personal responsibility, I've decided to make open questions a part of my life because it takes others into account. It prevents me from unconsciously guiding others in a direction for which I can potentially judge them afterward.

Open questions are better when it comes to building relationships and trust. If 80 percent of our questions are open and 20 percent are closed, we are in the right ballpark when it comes to connecting with others. The challenge is how to actually make this transition. It's not easy; it comes with habit. Yet there are some tricks we will learn in the next chapters.

Lesson: Good questions open the door to deeper connection.

Exercise 21: Flip the Script

Change the following closed questions into open questions. If you need help, the answers are in the back of the book.

Closed Question	Open Question
"Is this a good book?"	
"Are you well?"	
"Can you finish on time?"	
"Is it possible for you to do it?"	
"Are you looking forward to the trip?"	
"Can we see each other next week?"	

When we ask open questions, we invite deeper connection into our lives. Beyond that, we begin to understand people and situations better because we are not confining our questions to our biases. We learn a lot more when we do not push the conversation in a direction but rather invite the other to share what is really going on for them. When we begin to ask more open questions, we create a new world of seeing others and the world around us.

CHAPTER 22

The Process Is More Important than the Content

I have found that living a life guided by questions is very much like adopting improvisation as a lifestyle. If you go to an improvisation class, the rule is to always say yes to what another suggests. This requires one to be nimble on their feet and not directive in their actions. If someone yells out something absurd, you can't say, "No, say something else." You just roll with it.

The challenge when asking questions is that we cannot know what we are going to ask ahead of time. We prepare for the moment by being comfortable asking questions, not by knowing what specific ones we are going to ask. Of course, we can hold a few areas that are interesting to us in the back of our minds, but asking prepared questions is not going to create connection.

To create peace with this, we have to be comfortable with making mistakes. Having said this, I actually don't believe we can make mistakes, because anything we say can be cleaned up afterward with an apology and the next question. Which leads me to a very important distinction: process versus content. I discuss this often because it's one of the simplest ways I know to understand the difference between a transactional conversation and a dialogue. It also has helped me understand better how these two very different ways of interacting look and feel.

If we are concerned about content, then we seek knowledge.

The more we know, the more we can say. We're focused on what the person said and what we can say in response.

In a process, we are not interested with the content as much as we are the process between the people interacting. If we focus on the process of how we interact with someone, we're more conscious of what is said and how it might make sense to proceed from here.

I often tell people, "I am not really listening to you. Rather, I'm listening to how I feel as I hear you." I feel into what comes up in me as you speak and what that tells me about myself and my ideas of you and what you're sharing. This is what guides my questions. The skill is learning to ask meaningful questions. The art is hearing the voices in my head and connecting them to those questions.

As someone speaks, we notice thoughts in our heads—judgments, images, experiences. Not all of these thoughts are important. To determine which are important, the best criteria is to ask, "Is this something that interests or supports the other?" Usually, we'll find that our thoughts are stories from our pasts. It's not necessarily bad to share those stories, but we should consider the process we are in with another.

By telling a story, does it help the other person connect with themselves? Does it bring the two of us closer together? Or are we telling the story because we want to be seen and heard or to show they are not alone as we have the same background? We must be the judge, but it's always nice to default to uncertainty and not share. If we are good listeners, there will be tons of things we don't mention, even if we are dying to.

I often refer to this as surrendering to the process: allowing myself to let go of everything I know (content) and shift my attention to the moment (process). There are some best practices to make the process easier. Among the most important are deepening questions. A deepening question follows up from whatever the person said prior.

For example, a friend might be telling me a story and say, "We were having a great time, and then, all of a sudden, it changed."

A good deepening question could be, "What changed?" I take a single word from what the person said and ask them to deepen their understanding of it. It moves them to deepen their understanding of what occurred.

If instead I responded, "What did he say?" I'd be adding something that was not mentioned: "He said." By asking my friend this, it pulls her away from what she just said. I often say this is "putting them in their heads." They have to think in order to answer your question, instead of staying in the moment.

The intention in this process is to support people to stay with their emotions. To feel the struggle and move through it. With deepening questions, we're not trying to guide a person anywhere but deeper into their own emotions and process.

In the example above, we can see how easy it is to ask a deepening question. We select a word based on judgment ("good," "bad, "too much," etc.) or understatement of a complicated subject ("something happened," "there was a problem," "we had a hiccup," etc.). In all these cases, something is being said, but there is a lot more that has not been said. A deepening question brings out what has not been said, which is what the person is *really* concerned with.

Statement: "I've been eating way too much."
Deepening question: "What do you mean, 'too much?'"
Statement: "She never listens to me."
Deepening question: "How is that for you?"

When it comes to deepening questions, there is a simple way to cheat. I know I am breaking one of my own fundamental rules about staying authentic, but we have to start somewhere. People want to speak, so, preferably, questions will not disrupt a process. The simplest deepening question to ask is, "What else?"

"He said that he was going to make problems."
"And what else?"

"I don't even know what to do."

"And what else?"

People will generally take the question and make sense of it in their own minds. Whatever way they take the question is perfect. We are not guiding the content. We are supporting the process. If they take the question in an entirely different direction, we go with it. Remember, it's improvisation.

This can be challenging for people as they must let go of the idea that they can guide a conversation. And yet by letting go, we switch from a transactional conversation into a much deeper level of connection.

Another type of deepening question, which takes a bit more effort, uses observation. If we are listening, people will always give us clues into what's happening inside them.

"I notice you are getting teary eyed. What's going on?"

"Your voice changed. Is something coming up for you?"

In these examples, I do my best not to interpret what I'm observing. For instance, I don't say, "Why are you sad?" or, "You're nervous. Why?" Although those questions may continue the process, they also have the potential to trigger a reaction if the person is anxious or unable to connect with that feeling. In the worst cases, people tend to justify why they don't feel that way and then go back into their heads. It's not easy to bring them back.

There's a reason for that. Although it feels good to connect with our emotions, it's challenging to be vulnerable. A moment of levity is often used as an opportunity to move away from the emotions we are uncomfortable showing.

In addition to noticing things in others, we can also use things we notice in ourselves to form questions—thoughts that arise, emotions that get triggered. This can also help form a deepening question.

"I notice that I'm feeling uncomfortable. How is it for you?"

"I see that my palms are sweating. How are you doing?"

Again, notice in these examples that I am not asking the other directly. I'm sharing my experience and asking for theirs. This works best in large groups. In a group setting, when things get intense, there's a feeling in the room like a balloon filling up with pressure. For some, this pressure becomes too much, and they crack a joke or shift to a lighter subject. To allow the process to unfold, one must make comfort with tension, sadness, and, as mentioned earlier, silence.

✳ ✳ ✳

Lesson: Focus on the process, not the content.

Exercise 22: Dig Deeper

One of the best tools to deepen a relationship is deepening questions. To practice this, we will be doing the Dig Deeper exercise. How far down the well can you go when it comes to asking your questions? In each of the following sentences, see if you can spot the word or clue to a deepening question. Write down what you feel the next best question would be.

He was totally out of control.

"Out of control how?"

_____

She didn't know what she was doing.

"What was she doing?"

_____

The family is living beyond its means.

_____

He is too logical.

_____

They don't make a good couple.

_____

The project is bound to fail.

_____

Asking deepening questions is easy if we don't overthink it. We catch a word that has judgment attached to it or something that has a lot of meaning that has not been expressed. Alternatively, we can make an observation, as long as we don't interpret too much around it. You'd be shocked at how far a dialogue can go by simply taking single words or pointing out observations and asking a deepening question.

CHAPTER 23

Connect with Compassion

We've spent a lot of time on the importance of questions in deepening relationships. However, it's critical to understand that the energy and intention behind a question is far more important than the question itself. We can screw up the phrasing of a question but still make a connection if we get the intention right.

The emotion attached to questions that connect is compassion. Compassion involves feeling the emotions of the other while simultaneously feeling your own emotions.

Compassion is not empathy. Empathy is showing sympathy for another. It is touching a person on the shoulder when they are suffering and saying, "I'm sorry you are feeling this way." It's showing that we are aware of another's plight and offering some sort of support.

Although there are certainly overlaps with empathy and compassion, I'd like to offer a distinction. To help, I share a story. When I was twenty-three years old, my close friend's brother committed suicide. It was four years after my mother died, and I felt the pain he must have been going through.

I remember jumping in my car and driving to the basketball court where he was playing a game of pickup with people I did not know. I jumped over the fence and ran up to him in the middle of the game. I did not say a word or try to console him. I just walked right up to him and hugged him. We both cried. This is the feeling of compassion.

Twenty-five years later, he wrote me a long, heartfelt letter and told me that this single act changed his life forever. In that moment, he realized he was not alone. What I did on that court was allow him to experience my feelings. He saw in my eyes that I could see him. It was clear that words would only dampen the experience of being with someone who felt with him. I showed him not only that I felt sorry for his situation but also that I felt the depth of that loss in myself.

After my mom died, I longed for someone to see me. That did not mean that I wanted people to console me. I did not want to hear people telling me they were sorry for me or, "She is in a better place." I wanted to see my loss reflected in their eyes. I wanted them to look at me and acknowledge the pain. Not the pain of my loss but the pain of their own loss so that I could see that they understood mine. Not in words. In their presence.

That is compassion. If we want to have a meaningful dialogue, then we must connect with the compassion inside us. We do not need to have the same experience of loss, pain, grief, joy, or pride the other has experienced. That would be impossible, as we all have very different life experiences. But we can connect to our emotional equivalent.

There are thousands of ways to ask, "How are you?" How we ask this question will define what happens afterward. Whatever the other hears in our voices will set the atmosphere for the talk. Is the tone upbeat, looking for recognition of how they are doing? Is it empathetic, showing we are aware of something that is going on in their lives? Or is it compassionate, where the other feels totally seen as we show ourselves through the question and lets their guard down completely?

Imagine seeing an emotionally shutdown man staring at the floor as he walks past you, and you say, "How are you?" Delivered without expression, that question doesn't touch his emotions.

Now imagine you know he has recently lost someone he loves. You look him in the eyes and with a soft, compassionate voice say, "How are you?" Delivered with genuine compassion that the other can feel, that question alone can impact people so much that tears emerge and they have the opportunity to heal. We ask the question in this way to create space—to lower a person's guard and help them open up to their own emotions.

I'd like to repeat that to make a connection with compassion, we do not need to have the same life experience. It can certainly help, but it is not required. What we do need is to feel the emotions buried within us, the ones that may even prompt tears. Once we connect with that space and begin, the interaction quickly turns meaningful.

If you struggle with understanding compassion as I'm explaining it, then think for a moment. Have you ever had someone look at you and you just knew they truly understood you? Why did you feel that? Because you recognized the same emotion in them. They did not talk about it or explain it. They embodied it. You saw a knowingness in their eyes. That knowingness is compassion for the feelings you are having.

Compassion asks a lot of us, especially to feel. That's not easy for some, which is why I sometimes give more literal sentences in this book. We certainly do not need to say, "I know your mom died last month. How are you doing?" If we can look deeply into another person's eyes and feel the depth of our own pain while saying, "How are you doing?" our emotion alone will connect the other to their emotions.

Until now, I have mentioned compassion in relation to sadness. But there is a whole lot more to compassion. Imagine a friend who has achieved something big, like writing a book, buying a house, or winning a competition. Compassion would look different in each of these situations, but the underlying premise does not change. The other sees the emotions they are experiencing mirrored in our eyes, in our bodies—dare I say, in our vibrations. It's palpable.

It's the difference between saying with no emotion, "So how does it feel to own a house?" and "How does it feel to own a house?" with a softer voice, showing acknowledgment and recognition. Although the question might be exactly the same, the answer will be totally different.

In the emotionless question, the person asked does not feel seen, so the question pushes them to their logic. In the compassion-filled question, the emotion is pushed to the heart, and the person responds in kind.

I've often had moments where after a compassionate question, people share so much and yet are unaware of what has happened. That's how strong compassion is as an emotion. When people feel it, it opens them up and changes them in ways that they are not accustomed to and don't understand yet.

My friend's son recently graduated from college, and he was about to start looking for a job. I flashed back to my emotional state when I had just finished college and didn't know what I was going to do. I felt the helplessness, the anxiety, the indecision. I asked him with the deepest of compassion, "How are you feeling?" That single question led to an hour-long decompression as he let out all the weight of the thoughts he had been carrying while putting on a brave face to the world.

If you take away just one thing from this book, let it be this: if you can find compassion within yourself at the start of any important conversation, you are much more likely to have a meaningful connection. I should also say that you do not need to stay with compassion; merely begin there. It opens the heart up. If you continue with compassion, it will get a bit overwhelming for the other. So ask your opening question with compassion, and then allow empathy to guide you from there.

Lesson: Compassionate questions trigger deep emotions.

Exercise 23: Four Dimensions

For this exercise, you will repeat the same question four times, each with a deepening dimension of emotion. To help you reflect on the emotion, there is a short description next to each dimension. If you'd like some feedback, try it out with a partner and hear how the questions are impacting them. Don't worry if you find it challenging—because it is.

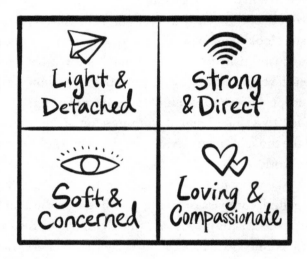

Dimension 1: **Light and detached** (like you are saying it without attaching to the words).

Dimension 2: **Strong and direct** (like you are asking to get a response).

Dimension 3: **Soft and concerned** (like you know something is not going well and you are concerned).

Dimension 4: **Loving and compassionate** (like you feel your own emotions deeply when you ask).

"How are you?"

"How were the results?"

"What's your plan for the future?"

"When are you going to decide?"

How we ask questions will have a great impact on how they are received. The more compassionate they are, the deeper they will be felt, and the more likely they will create a deeper connection. If you are just learning how to bring emotion into your questions, take it slow and reflect on the feedback you receive. It is a process that begins with a first step.

LISTEN TO THE
CHAPTER

CHAPTER 24

The Power of Touch

Although this book is primarily about the speaking part of communications, it's important to note other powerful forms of communication. Eye contact and touch, for example, are two superpowers that justify having their own chapter.

I realized the power of touch through watching a friend support a couple. As the partners bickered back and forth, the friend asked the two to turn toward one another, hold one another's hands, and continue again.

What happened changed my understanding of touch forever. They followed his instructions, and the dynamic changed entirely. Everything softened. As the two held hands, they could not maintain the angry state they had been trapped in just seconds earlier. Their voices gentled. Each started to use the word "I" to begin each sentence instead of "you." "I feel uncomfortable when you say that" instead of "You always say that!" It was as if I were looking at two entirely different people. This fascinating display has stayed with me ever since.

It taught me how easy it is to demonize a person when we are detached from them. Once we touch their hand, it's really hard to pretend they are not also human, imperfect, and struggling.

As with most things that we understand through our own experience, there are studies that give us insight into why this is true. One such study used romantic couples to look at the effects of touch on pain. Neuroscientists devised an experiment where one partner was placed into an fMRI machine while holding the other's hand. The partner in the machine was then given a painful stimulation. The results revealed that hand-holding reduced the pain of the one receiving stimulation compared to people in the control group, who held a rubber ball.[4] That's the power of touch!

We often get so caught up in our own suffering that it's easy to forget we are not alone. That we are not the only ones feeling pain. It's easy to see the world through the filter of "me versus you" when we're physically separated. Touching forces us to stop that separation. Touching brings the reality of our words and how they impact another into our consciousness. It stops hurtful ways of speaking by connecting us to the humanity of the other and makes it harder to project negatively on those we are challenged by.

In my coaching practice, when I feel things getting out of control, I will ask the couple to face one another and hold hands. For some, this is not easy as it forces a new awareness in each that it's not just about themselves.

Complementary to touch and possibly even more powerful is eye gazing. I tuned in to the power of eye gazing when I lived in Japan for two years.

As an American, I was taught to look people in the eyes when I spoke with them. It was a sign of respect and showed that I could be trusted. It was a way of standing in one's strength. In Japan, eye contact signified quite the opposite. Looking directly into another's eyes was considered confrontational, inconsiderate, even rude. In that environment, I saw for the first time that there was something penetrating about looking directly into someone's eyes. Eye gazing is a combination of simultaneously revealing one's own mask and seeing through the mask of the other.

In my time in Japan, I adapted and learned to avoid eye contact. When I returned to Europe, I was again confronted with the reverse. I now found it challenging to look people in the eyes. I remember being taken aside by a business partner after we had become friends, and he told me, "It took me years to trust you because you never looked me in the eyes." I immediately remembered the shift I had made in Japan, and I laughed as I shared with him the story of how challenging it was to adapt into and out of cultural norms.

During my first eye-gazing exercise at a seminar, I was asked to partner with a woman whom I had just met ten minutes earlier. She was in her forties, and I could tell she was nervous. She was giggly and a bit jumpy.

We were instructed to spend ten minutes looking into one another's eyes without averting our gaze and without speaking. The instructions were to just "make your eyes available to one another." The first few minutes were uncomfortable. I didn't know exactly where to look, and I found myself picking out points in her eye to stare at. She continued to giggle, until there was a sudden shift in both of us.

As I relaxed into the exercise, I began to stare less and simply hold my eyes in a state of connection. Once in this state, my perception shifted. Time slowed. I felt her slowly melt away and gained a sense of shapelessness. It ended with a moment that I will never forget, as I shifted my sense of being and went from looking at her to seeing myself through her eyes. It was trippy, almost as if this were a psychedelic experience. This experience impacted her as well; tears began to fall from her eyes. In the end, we hugged and felt a deep connection, which we have kept to this day.

I learned a few lessons from this experience. The most important is that there is a power in looking someone in the eyes with an open heart. But what has stayed with me ever since goes beyond eye gazing and has to do more with how I look at the world. In the eye-gazing exercise, in the moment before I surrendered to the exercise, my eyes were fixed and directed, looking for something to focus on. I equate this with the eyes of a predator looking for prey, directed straight ahead. These are the eyes of focus, determination, control. The eyes of someone wanting something from another.

When I surrendered to the exercise, my eyes changed. They became the eyes of the prey. Softer, more open, more accessible. Absorbing the entire picture and not focusing on any single part. These are the eyes of a person who wants nothing from another except to connect. I have since come to refer to these as "soft eyes." I equate them with the state of compassion I mentioned in the prior chapter. These eyes are mirrors to the soul for others who look into them.

In alternating looking at the world through the eyes of the predator or prey, I notice that I have a very different view. As the predator, I try to figure out what I am seeing. As the prey, I absorb and let my stomach guide me. This translates directly into our relations because when people see in our eyes the desire to be present and absorb, they are more likely to be vulnerable and reveal themselves to us. This is not surprising; who would want to leave themselves open to a predator?

* * *

Lesson: When all else fails, take a person's hand and look them straight in the eyes.

Exercise 24: Eyes to the Soul

For the most part, you can get through this book without depending on another. All of the previous exercises can be done alone. But in this next exercise, you will need to find someone to share this experience with.

Sit down comfortably across from one another, facing your partner with nothing between you. Set a timer for five minutes. Prepare to gaze into the eyes of your partner. This is not a staring competition, so you are free to blink.

If you get distracted, don't worry. It's normal at first. Just bring your awareness back to the eyes of your partner.

When you're done, connect with your partner in the way that feels most comfortable and share how the experience was for both of you. If this is the first time you have done this, then don't worry if the experience was uncomfortable or not impactful.

RECAP

It's easy to forget that the people we are angry or frustrated with are also human and going through their own pain. In the moments when we feel ourselves separating from them, we can reach out and touch them, looking them in the eyes to remind ourselves that we are both human. In this state of connection, we are better able to see one another and soften the tension.

SECTION VI

Navigating Tricky Connections

CHAPTER 25

Handling "Difficult Discussions"

You might understand everything I've written so far—but then the overwhelming "difficult discussion" rears its head. It's like training for a climb by taking a comfortable nature walk and then, all of a sudden, without notice, we are standing in front of Mount Everest. Knowing all the ways to climb via a book does not prepare us for the ascent.

As a coach, I often get calls from people asking me how to handle impending difficult conversations. "It's one of the hardest things I've ever done." "What am I going to say?" These are the phrases I hear over and over again as people imagine the agony to come. As I'm very sensitive, I hear all these sentences in my body. Can *you* feel what happens to yourself as you say these things? Can you feel the constriction? Can you sense the impending doom? In my case, my throat constricts, I feel heavy in my head, and my stomach tightens.

Take a moment and consider: how does looking at a situation in such a way prime our minds? Or, going back to an earlier lesson, how does the fact that I have primed myself to believe that it will be a difficult discussion actually turn it into a difficult discussion? I have found that difficult discussions often occur because we frame them that way.

The fight-or-flight defenses of the brain's amygdala—where our responses for fear, anxiety, and aggression are stored—is already active. What's going to happen? When is the pain going to come? In this state of mind, an emotion lurks under each word. We worry that the other is reading, either consciously or unconsciously, what we are emitting. For lack of better word, we emit a vibration that's palpable to people around us, even if we think that it's not. As a dear friend once told me, "You can hide, but you can't hide that you're hiding."

Telling ourselves that we're going into a difficult discussion is actually the biggest challenge we face. Let's play a mind experiment. Imagine I'm going to introduce you to someone. But before I do, I tell you, "She told me she doesn't like you." You go to shake her hand. How does it feel? Probably not good.

Let's switch the scene. The same situation, but this time I tell you, "She told me what a great person you are." Now shake her hand. How is it different? Can you feel your body relax? Your eyes soften? An involuntary smile?

These are cues that set the stage for how a conversation will proceed. It reminds me of the famous quote, "A boxing match is decided before the boxers ever enter the ring." The mental preparation and mind games at the weigh-in will set one boxer's mind into doubt, and at that moment, they lose the upper edge. They may be the better boxer, but they'll often lose the fight.

When approaching a potentially difficult discussion, the first trick is to not view it as a difficult discussion, thereby relaxing our system and enabling us to think more clearly.

Once we're relaxed, we prepare for the possibility of what I call a "possible no-match discussion." By this I mean that there are some situations where we simply won't be able to come to terms with another person. Our mindset and intentions do not align. By referring to it as a "possible no-match discussion" versus a "difficult discussion," we immediately place our mind in a wholly different state.

When approaching a difficult discussion, our mindset is often fearful and adversarial. We're likely attached to the other person understanding and agreeing with us, or at least attached to the idea of a resolution we both feel good about.

This may or may not be possible. So instead of being attached to an outcome and assuming the conversation is going to be difficult, we simply ask if there is a match in how we will continue working together, how we will continue our relationship, or how we each perceive the project is being managed.

In this mindset, the other person can feel that we have not predetermined an outcome we're pushing for. We're not directing them. We're also not judging them but simply pointing out the things we've observed. By priming ourselves for a possible no-match discussion versus a difficult discussion, we've immediately made the discussion impersonal. The words "You did that" are replaced with "I saw that . . ." This turns it from an accusation into an observation.

However, it's not easy. In order to shift our mindset and be at peace with simply observing, we also have to see our judgments toward this person and make peace with those judgments. In this case, we use the self-acceptance exercise I detailed in Chapter 9.

In a nutshell, we are driven by what we avoid. The trick I've learned is to not resist it but rather embrace it completely, without shame or guilt. This might sound like, "This person is going to be totally unreasonable, and it's okay." Or, "I hate this person, and it's fucking great." In embracing this, we calm that voice of judgment in our heads, and it is less likely to drive us during our contact.

Once we've primed our mind, made peace with our judgment, and prepared ourselves to point out a possible no-match, we've created the conditions for a productive discussion to emerge.

The moment comes. We shake the other's hand, and they feel our calm. Since we are not judging them, we look them in the eyes and show them we are at peace with the subject matter. We begin to point out the things that are not working.

"I don't feel that you are able to fulfill your role. You have promised three deadlines that have not been met."

"Yes, but it was not my fault. The other team did not deliver what I needed."

"Yes, I understand that. But as the project manager, it's your job to let us know this ahead of time. It would not have been a problem had you told us two weeks ago."

"But I did not know this two weeks ago. They just told me."

I interrupt this conversation here because I'd like to show a typical moment where people get frustrated. The project manager does not take any responsibility for what has happened. Blame ensues, which deflects responsibility. It's easy to let frustration guide the conversation from here. That would be a shame, though, because this is the moment to continue with questions.

"So, help me understand. As project manager, how could you get a better indication if they are not going to make the deadline in the future? How could you escalate it differently so it does not turn into a problem next time? What might you do differently so we are not having this same conversation next week?"

In the above example, I am presuming that we do not want to end this person's employment but would prefer to see an improvement in their behavior. If this were to happen over and over again, the discussion would be very different.

"John, I see that this is the fourth time we have had this discussion, and you are not giving me any other choice. As I told you in our last conversation, if this happens again, we will have to let you go, and it has happened again. It feels terrible, but given the circumstances, we don't have an alternative. What we need is not getting done, and we need a change."

I use this scenario because in business, when we have exhausted all other possibilities, the consequence is letting a person go. We cannot pretend otherwise; that would not be fair to them or us. There is certainly a place where this person can flourish. It just happens that this business is not that place.

Difficult discussions are such because they are emotionally challenging. How we make peace with ourselves before, during, and after these discussions shifts how we engage others and thereby shifts the energy and outcome of our discussions. In my own experience, I'm still very close with people I've had to fire. It's never been personal, for the most part. There just wasn't a match.

Understanding all this is also important for ourselves and for when we're supporting others who are about to enter difficult conversations. We can't tell someone with a charged system to "relax." That usually compounds the problem because now we have made them aware that they are conspicuously nervous.

The first thing I do is make sure that the other's nervousness does not penetrate my psyche. It's easy to get drawn into this state, so making sure my body and mind are settled is important.

It's hard to realize the moment we've become nervous as a result of our environment. Think of the story of the frog in boiling water. If we toss a frog into a vat of boiling water, it will jump out immediately. If we put it in tepid water and heat the water progressively, it will remain until it boils. Nervousness is the boiling water. As others grow more and more nervous, they begin to penetrate our psyches, and the water gets hotter.

This may seem at odds with compassion. In meaningful conversations, aren't we *supposed* to feel compassion for what another is feeling? In this case, reflecting another person's nervousness is not helpful. They are feeling nervous because of their unseen assumptions and judgments. If we climb into that box with them, we are unable to support them, because now we're feeling the same things they are.

In this case, it helps to have a healthy detachment by not buying into their assumptions. This way, we can more clearly help them see how they are priming themselves to have a difficult discussion. We can support them by showing them the calm energy that comes from becoming aware of assumptions and making peace with judgment.

The key to handling difficult discussions is to deal with our mindsets, assumptions, judgments, and energy before going into the discussion. With this preparation, we can make the discussion less personal, which makes it much more likely that the discussion will be productive and connective.

✳ ✳ ✳

Lesson: Difficult discussions are made more difficult by assuming they will be.

Exercise 25: Staring Down the Barrel

In this chapter, the focus has been on how assuming a conversation will be difficult often makes it so. It is not easy to change this mindset, but the following exercise may help.

Think of a special person in your life. The one who makes your hairs stand on end. The dread of speaking with them alone makes you anxious.

In your imagination, look at this person and take in every emotion that comes up when you think of the discussion that is about to occur. Shift your attention to all the judgment you have for that person.

Write down the specific ways in which you judge this person (e.g., "He/She is difficult. He/She is unreasonable," etc.).

Now use the self-acceptance tool in Chapter 9 and make peace with all of your judgments of this person by settling them in your system. For example, "He is difficult, and it's okay." "She is unreasonable, and it's okay." Be exhaustive with every judgment you have of this person.

After settling these judgments, we need to separate your *observations* of this person's behavior from your *interpretations* of his or her behavior. For example, "He often shows up late to meetings" is an observation. "He does not respect me" is an interpretation. "She has failed to meet her targets four times in a row" is an observation. "She is incompetent" is an interpretation.

To continue, the next page has two words written as headers ("Observation" and "Interpretation") with a line down the middle.

I want you to take a moment and think about everything this person has done wrong and put it on one side of the column or the other. If you sense judgment toward the person, put it in the right-hand column. If it is an observation (void of a value judgment), put it in the left-hand column.

For all items in the right-hand column, take a moment and write what you have observed to make you come to that judgment. As you do this, sense how your judgments soften as you turn them into observations.

In this mindset of a possible no-match discussion, you are not confronting this person with judgments but rather pointing out the things you've observed and asking questions like, "How are we going to change this?" "What can we do to make sure that this never happens again?" "What comes up for you as I share this?"

When you reflect on that possible discussion, how does it feel? How do you see yourself interacting differently, compared to if you stated your opinions and judgments?

❶ Write down your judgements of ___	❷ Make peace with it	❸ Which is it?
Ex. He is difficult!	And that's okay.	○ Observation ☑ Interpretation
	And that's okay.	○ Observation ○ Interpretation
	And that's okay.	○ Observation ○ Interpretation
	And that's okay.	○ Observation ○ Interpretation

❹ Judgement ⟶	Observation
Ex. **He is difficult!**	I have trouble interacting with him.

RECAP

We can lighten the load on our minds if we assume that people are good and they sometimes do "bad things." Turning our judgments of people into observations gives us the opportunity to bring them forward impersonally. This does not guarantee that a discussion will be painless, but it gives us the best shot at getting there. And remember, you can always go back and use this exercise to prepare for a possible no-match discussion in the future.

CHAPTER RECAP VIDEO

LISTEN TO THE CHAPTER

CHAPTER 26

Sorry Opportunities

One of the lessons I cherish most from my mentor, Cees, is to stop viewing situations in life as mistakes that cannot be fixed. I remember exactly what he said to me: "Every problem is an opportunity in disguise. Don't move away from it. Move toward it. It's a process with no beginning or end. Just use this moment as another reason to connect."

Some of the best moments to create connection actually come after we have seemingly made big mistakes.

Like with many things discussed in this book, the challenge is not logical but rather requires an entire change in mindset. We must be open to letting go of the inner voice that says, "You screwed up. It's better to move on from this relationship." It's never easy to sit with an apparent screwup; it hurts. And no one wants to sit in pain for too long. It's easier to say, "I lost this time" and move on.

I was once coaching a business client who shared a situation that she thought was unfixable.

"What's so bad that it can't be solved with an apology?" I asked.

She replied, "Well, I sent an email out to my manager, telling him that I was only using a small percentage of my time working on the business. Given that I'm earning a lot of money, it did not go well."

"I can imagine that," I said. "It must have been difficult for him to hear you're only spending a fraction of your time focusing on the business. My question is, is that really true?"

"No, not really," she admitted.

"So why did you say it?" I asked.

She answered, "I did not want to feel guilty if I spent time on another project, so I exaggerated the actual amount of time. I only realized afterward that that was a mistake."

"It feels like you're trying to sabotage yourself," I observed. "It's as if you don't want to make the decision to leave, so you are hoping to force an outcome."

"Yes, I can certainly see that," she said.

I continued, "I can't tell you if it makes sense to leave. That's clearly your decision. What I can say is that I'd prefer that it was not done as a reaction to fear. I'd prefer it to be something you're moving toward, not something you're moving away from. If you don't address it here, then it will only show up again the next time you are feeling uncomfortable about something."

"What do you suggest I do?" she asked.

I said, "I've often found that there are no real mistakes. We are in a process. And at this step of the process, there is probably confusion, tension, and a bit of anger. These are not bad things. In fact, I find that if you don't go through this process, you often aren't able to reorganize things in a different way."

"What do you mean by that?" she asked.

"Well, change is never easy. It often takes an outside impetus. That can come in many forms—health issues, death, bankruptcy. Or in your case, an email. That email is now creating tension. How that tension gets resolved is the question we are now sitting with."

"I see."

"And the best way I see to resolve the tension you've created is through vulnerability and context."

"What do you mean?" she asked.

"In your original email, you told your boss what you were feeling. It felt vulnerable, but it was only the outside layer of the onion. If you want to move people, then you must let them see a few layers deeper."

"How do I do that?"

"Well, why were you sabotaging yourself?"

"Because I was afraid he would not understand."

"And why were you afraid of that?"

"It's a pattern in my life. When I don't feel as if I'm going to be seen, I act from fear and push people away before they can do the same to me."

"So if you wanted to create clarity with your boss and possibly improve the relationship, what could you do?"

"I guess I would share with him what was really going on when I sent the message so he could better understand why I wrote it."

"You guess?" I prodded.

"I say that because I'm still not sure I want to work there."

"That I understand," I said. "But at least when it comes to making sure you stay in connection with him, there is no harm in sending that message. At least, none that I see."

"Yes, I got it," she said.

Looking at this interaction, we see the moment when my client acted from a disconnected state. This is very typical. We say things that are less than ideal or make decisions that don't pan out. Then we are left with the reality.

If we try to make sense of it through justification, we remain stuck in our heads. It can be exhausting trying to figure out why we did something and what we can do differently in the future. This mindset appears to open the mind but actually shuts it down.

The question is not how to do it better in the future. The question is, "What's really going on inside of me now? How has this impacted my behavior and therefore the people around me?" In answering those questions and sharing those answers openly, we heal and draw people closer to us. Even in the worst situations.

In my own life, Christmas has always been a difficult holiday for me. It was my mother's favorite day, so every year I'm reminded of how much I miss her. As I was never able to share this openly, or even fully feel it myself, I would shut down emotionally every Christmas.

During one Christmas season, I was at a girlfriend's house with her family, and the simplest situation triggered me. I bought a gift for my girlfriend that I wanted to keep a secret. Her family disregarded this and told her. In the emotional state I was in, I took it personally. I got angry and grabbed my shoes, hoping to get out the door and run away from the pain. The situation was exaggerated for such a small thing, but I was in so much pain that I exploded and needed to get out.

This left the family in disarray. My behavior created confusion and commotion. Then it hit me. I saw my mom's face and realized where the pain was coming from. The pain I was avoiding. I called everyone into the kitchen and shared everything. How painful Christmases were for me. How being with a happy family reminded me of everything I lost with my mom's death. The house went from discord to connection in a moment. It was the most beautiful Christmas of my life because I allowed myself to be seen.

In that moment, I was vulnerable and I gave context. Both are required. If I was only vulnerable, then they would have felt me but still been confused as to what created the outburst to begin with. If I gave the context but was not vulnerable, then they might have understood me intellectually but would not have been able to feel the depth of what it really meant to me and then connect with me.

When something goes wrong in a relationship, we have the opportunity to share what's *really* going on in a way that allows people to understand and appreciate us even more than before. This translates into business and personal life, as we see from the two examples provided. We always have the opportunity to move from what feels like a bad situation and turn it into a deeply meaningful moment.

✳ ✳ ✳

Lesson: Mistakes in relationships are opportunities in disguise.

Exercise 26: Turn It Around

Choose the response below that you feel is most likely to turn around an uncomfortable situation. All of the answers are suitable, but one of them is best.

Situation ❶

You mistakenly press send on an email to a person with embarrassing information about them in it:

Ⓐ Hey, this message was not intended for you. Please ignore it.

Ⓑ Hello, I sent this email to you by mistake. Can we talk?

Ⓒ Hello, I sent you an email by mistake. I was hoping to get on a call with you. I see there are some things I wish I had not written.

Ⓓ I just sent you a stupid email. I wrote some things in it about you, and I realize now that was not right or fair. I'd be grateful if you'd be open to discussing it.

Situation ❷

A customer you have been working with for years tells you that they are canceling the contract and going to the competition.

Ⓐ As we have been working with you for years, I'd like to speak with you.

Ⓑ I completely understand that you have reasons to leave us. Would you be open to getting on a call so that I can better understand what we might be able to improve in the future?

Ⓒ I see that you have chosen to leave for another company. As I would like to keep you as a customer, I am sorry that you are leaving us.

Ⓓ Thank you for the years together. I am happy that we had the chance to serve you as long as we did.

Situation ❸

In the middle of an intense argument with a friend, you lose your cool and say something that hurts them deeply.

Ⓐ I know what I said was wrong, and I'm sorry.

Ⓑ I'd like to apologize for what I said. In the heat of the argument, it came out, and I did not mean it.

Ⓒ I'm so sorry I hurt you. I was feeling so much pain, and I lashed out. It was not right. I really wanted to hurt you because I felt like you were hurting me, and that was not right.

Ⓓ Although what you said was not kind, I should not have responded to you that way.

RECAP

Life is not always easy, and on occasion we do things that we regret afterward. When we step back from the situation, it is possible to see opportunities. When we let down our defenses and show ourselves, we invite a deeper connection and healing. It's important to remember that we are not sharing with the expectation of healing the relationship. We share because it gives us peace and it is one further step to taking personal responsibility in our own lives.

CHAPTER RECAP VIDEO

LISTEN TO THE CHAPTER

CHAPTER 27

Setting Healthy Boundaries

For many people, the most challenging aspect of communication is saying no. There are many emotions that can come up with this word, so it must be addressed with caution. A friend of mine once played an experimental game where he invited participants to yell, "No" repeatedly, and it ended in tears for many of the attendees.

"No" is loaded because of its close association with the incapacity to set boundaries. The inability to set boundaries often comes from people-pleasing behavior, and in my experience, it can be one of the hardest things to overcome. Once a people-pleaser associates "no" with rejection, they are trapped into believing that by saying no, they are rejecting another. Maybe someone they care deeply about. Since it doesn't feel good to reject someone, sadness and care is often attached to it.

It's essential to feel comfortable addressing "no" because, in a very real way, we become unreliable when we are unable to do so. The pattern looks something like this: We say yes to things that we don't have the time or capacity to do and then fail to deliver. This invariably gets compounded over time as more and more things are left open while more people ask for favors. Frustration builds with people we've made promises to, which increases stress and an incessant feeling of being behind. In my experience, this leads to burnout or health problems.

A dear friend of mine always asks how he can support me. I see how hard he works, so I am always cautious to add anything to his plate. Since he is the owner of a media company that could help me get my work to the world, I would love his support. However, I see his inability to say no not as an opportunity but rather as a liability, given that he is helping so many other people.

It has been my experience that such people can be unreliable because they are simply stretching themselves too far. I also know that when expectations are brought into a relationship, resentment can quickly grow. Expectations that are not fulfilled often lead to tension and blame.

As we are quite close, I sometimes act as a mentor and lovingly tease him, calling him my "unreliable friend." My teasing is not done to diminish him nor blame him. Rather, I aim to help him embrace the behavior, which he has told me he would like to change.

When taking on this subject, I feel some trepidation because our reasons for not saying no are very specific to each of us. As I mentioned, there is often deep trauma associated with the word. We might judge ourselves for the moments when we were unable to say no in the past. I have experienced the pain of people who were molested as children, and my heart breaks as I see the victim judge themselves for not being able to say no as a child, completely neglecting the role of the perpetrator.

For the purposes of this book, we are not dealing with this traumatic "no." The "no" we're looking at here occurs when we are confronted with someone whose behavior is impacting us in a way we do not want. When it comes to setting boundaries, the first question I always ask is, "Am I setting a boundary with someone I would like to stay in contact with, or would I prefer not to have contact with this person?"

This is an important question because how we interact with them will define our relationship going forward. There are many instances in my life where I have simply decided to not make space for people, and that is just fine. It is important to decide if we really want to have contact with a person or if we just want to push them away. In the latter case, it is less about setting a boundary and more about simply saying, "I'd rather not see you."

Now, let's presume for a moment that this is a person with whom we would like to remain in contact, as long as there is a change in behavior. The next question to ask is, "Am I judging the other and asking them to be something they are not so that I feel more comfortable around them?"

That would be less about setting a boundary and more about us not accepting this person for who they are. This goes back to the story of me and my wife when she showed no interest in attending any of the courses I was taking at the start of our relationship. I could have told her, "I am setting a boundary. You need to go to these courses, or we are going to break up." Thankfully, it never went that far. But you can see that in this instance, I would have been asking her to do something I wanted, using the idea of "boundary setting" to manipulate the situation.

The key is to understand that healthy boundaries are about saying no to behavior, not to the person. Going back to Chapter 13, it is essential when setting boundaries that we separate the personal from the impersonal.

For example, consider a person who constantly shows up late to appointments. The personal assumption would be, "He is so unreliable." The impersonal observation is, "He has showed up late five times this month." In the latter instance, we are pointing at the occurrences and not applying a value judgment. When we set a boundary, we are saying no to the behavior of showing up late, not trying to make the person become more reliable. Of course, if the person shows up on time, the natural consequence is that he becomes more reliable, but we do not focus on reliability—just the time.

The caution here is that once we set our mind in the frame of "setting a boundary," we are potentially pushing a person away, priming ourselves for a difficult discussion. Who wants to be told,

"You are doing something wrong, and you need to stop it"?

To make it less likely that I will alienate someone, I pay heed to the fact that for everything I do not want, there is an opposing side of what I *do* want. Taking the example of the person who shows up late, the negative version is, "I don't want him to show up late." The positive version is, "I want to start meetings on time."

When addressing boundaries, I focus on what I want and invite people to join me there. "I would love to start the meeting with everyone present. Without having everyone here, we are delayed." In this case, we are both pointing out the importance of starting on time and the consequences of not doing so. We are not actually setting a boundary; we are inviting a person to join us in this way of working. Of course, if this behavior repeats, we point it out and spell out the consequences for the team and eventually the person. In my experience, such issues are not usually resolved in a one-time discussion. They are a process that occurs over time. Patterns are not easy to break in others, so it is best to manage our own expectations.

This all leads to a point I have not yet addressed, which I call "reframing" or "recontextualizing." I am referring to the lens through which a person narrates something. When we set boundaries, we tend to narrate our story in a negative form: "I don't want this" or "I will not tolerate that." We might spend weeks, months, or even years building up frustration and resentment for all the things that we failed to say no to in the past. These experiences crystallize into a deep well of pain that we then refer to as our "boundary."

As I have repeated often in this book, this is not a problem. And in many ways, it is necessary, especially with deep trauma. But the more we frame a boundary as something that implies judgment of another, the more we push the other away. There are consequences for a boundary mindset.

To counter the potential negative consequences of a boundary mindset, I am conscious to narrate the story of what I want in a positive form, as shown above. By doing that, it very seldom becomes necessary to hold a boundary. Instead, the people who do not want to join me tend to naturally drop off. There is no blame in this, because I get to choose how I want to live, and the other has the same privilege.

How I narrate my life has direct consequences for situations where boundaries become necessary. My fundamental question is, "Do I invite or alienate?" There are hundreds of frames we can choose from when we narrate our lives and what we want, and each has a very different consequence. The frame we set as a narration defines us.

To make this more concrete, I will address some boundaries in the negative and then positive forms:

Situation: Mom continually asks me when I am going to get married.

"I am really tired of you asking about this. If you do this again, I am going to leave."

"Mom, you've asked me ten times over the last month when I am going to get married. I know you love me and you are asking because you are excited. But you putting pressure on me is only slowing things down. I would love for you to be supportive of my life, with or without marriage. It will make my life nicer if this is not always a discussion."

Situation: A friend was not honest.

"If you lie to me again, our relationship is over. This is a clear boundary."

"I know you were out with friends when you told me you were home. I don't mind that you went out. I do mind that you hid it from me. I would love to have friendships where we can talk about anything, especially the hard stuff."

Situation: I have an overly protective parent.

"I'm sick of you meddling in my life. This must stop now. If you continue pestering me, I won't be coming to visit again."

"I know you want the best for me and you are only trying to protect me. But your constant management of my life has to come to an end. I would like to see us interacting as friends and loving relations, not as the child you feel you still need to take care of."

In all the positive examples, you see that there is compassion for the other. We are acknowledging their humanity and at the same time expressing our desire in the form of an invitation. Although I have offered single statements above, variations of these statements would need to be repeated throughout the change process.

People often fall into the same old patterns a few times before a new behavior takes its place. Do not blame them. Simply go back to the phrases and say, "Remember we talked about this?" Sometimes patience is required. But in relationships that matter, I love to invite people to join me in something special so I don't carry the feeling that I am always managing them.

In cases where time is not an option, the phrases remain the same: "Remember we talked about this?" except we'd continue with something like, "And if this does not change, I will unfortunately need to separate for a while." Or, "I don't know how we can continue working together if this happens again."

In the end, it is always an invitation and a vision of how we would like things to go. If the other does not choose to join us, it simply was not meant to be.

✳ ✳ ✳

Lesson: Setting boundaries is an invitation for deeper connection.

Exercise 27: The Mirror Has Two Faces

One of the biggest challenges we can face in life is saying no. Sometimes we don't even see that there is also something we could say yes to. In the next exercise, you are asked to take the negative form of the sentence and reframe it in a positive form.

⚡ Facing Negative ⚡	♡ Facing Positive ♡
I don't want you to say that anymore.	I would like to be in a relationship where we commit to being loving.
I am sick of you telling me what to do.	I'd love if we could support one another to raise up, not tell one another what to do.
You are not listening to me.	I want both of us to feel listened to, and I will commit to doing my best.
You are not doing what we agreed to.	
You are talking nonsense.	

Translating what we don't want into what we do want is not always easy. We do this so that others have the opportunity to join us in our vision of how we'd like to live. In this way of living, there is no need to say no or push others away, because those who don't want to join us will decide for themselves. And if need be, we separate while holding love at the center of our contact. See how this shift feels, and notice the difference in your interactions.

CHAPTER RECAP VIDEO

CHAPTER 28

Seeing through False Pretenses

Everything good in life comes with a dark shadow. Connection is no different. The shadow side of connection comes in a few shapes and forms, but it can be recognized by its unquestioning belief that connection is "the answer." I've found that when people start out with anything new, they believe they have found the secret and want to share it, oblivious to the pain they're causing by not being fully developed in their understanding. And let me be clear: when managed unconsciously, the principle of connection can cause emotional damage to others.

Furthermore, there are individuals who might be unconscious of their intentions but are still highly skillful at using connection to manipulate and control others.

I once attended a training in Oregon. The head trainer had founded a large group with a focus on vulnerability. He had hosted hundreds of sessions and built up a name for himself. I was invited to join as part of a multiday training series, and I was happy to check out his work.

Throughout the course were exercises that created deep intimacy. One of them dropped people into a deep state of connection through eye gazing with a partner. The sensation is quite powerful, especially if one has never done it before. Deep emotions can arise. Oxytocin, often referred to as the "love hormone," can be triggered, and one is not even aware of why they have developed strong feelings for the person across from them.

After a few of these sessions, I noticed the trainer continually touching the women in the group. On the surface, it could be written off as the byproduct of the connection games that were played. But there was something more. A continuous flirting, which gave the feeling that he was looking to see who might be interested. A remark here, a flirtatious gaze there, a story to feign vulnerability with the hopes that a woman might hold him.

As it progressed, I realized that this was not a connection course but rather a way for the trainer to find hookups. To check, I spoke with a few of the women to better understand if there were any uncomfortable feelings coming up for them. Sure enough, there were.

I approached him and said, "Hey, Sean, I see you running these exercises, and it feels like you are using the emotions created here to connect with women sexually."

"Well, you can't stop sexual feelings from coming up," he said.

"Yes, that's clear," I said. "But my concern is that you are blind to the fact that you are now taking the beauty of this moment and channeling it to an expectation for sex."

He admitted, "I mean, that sometimes happens, but it's just what happens at these types of events."

"Sean, it may be what happens, but you are not considering the potential consequences. This may be the first time a person has felt connected. A trust has been created in this setting. They are letting their guard down. It may be the hardest thing they've ever done, and now they are vulnerable. When you have sex with them in that moment, it could very well traumatize that person for the rest of their life."

He defended, "It's not like I am forcing anyone to do anything. We are all adults here."

It was clear that he did not want to understand my point. If he did, it would mean that he'd have to change, and that was not something he was interested in doing. Sean was using vulnerability as a tool to attract people to him—possibly to find a woman with caretaking instincts in the group who would show him love and maybe a bit more.

These types of trainers are, frankly, dangerous. Connection is one of our deepest human needs. When we dig into this well of our subconscious, powerful emotions arise that need to be integrated. By integrated I mean they need time to find a place in our system where they all feel grounded.

Creating these "peak experiences" without any concrete integration moving forward completely removes the value from the experience. People often get addicted to the emotional highs they experience in seminars. This is not a bad thing. In fact, I love joining a course here and there, if just to feel my blood circulate. But the responsibility of the trainer cannot be underestimated. And when the trainer's unconscious desires bleed into the training, run for the exits.

The tricky part in these cases is that many people are enamored with the perpetrator because he or she presents themselves vulnerably. This is a trap. Just because one presents themselves vulnerably does not mean their intentions are coming from a clean place.

Vulnerability means surrendering to an emotion—letting that emotion be acknowledged and seen by others. It's not done for show or theatrics. It's done because that is the genuine feeling at that moment. When someone knows that by showing an emotion, they will get comforted, that is not vulnerability. That is manipulation.

It's not easy to look at someone crying and say, "Stop the act." That's a surefire way of making a lot of enemies. Instead, I fall back on the same exercise I've mentioned repeatedly in this book. The structure is "Observation (without judgment) + Open Questions (without guidance)."

Picking back up on conversation with Sean, I said, "I see that you don't want to hurt anyone. So how do you make sure that people who are very vulnerable don't feel taken advantage of afterward?"

Sean's eyes softened, and his eyes watered as he said, "I've also got my shadows. It's not like I'm perfect. And yes, I do like making deeper connections with people in these sessions."

I had the feeling that by crying, he was hoping I'd step back. The crying was a defense. Others were watching, and I saw him once again gathering sympathy—and that I'd become the "bad one" for making him cry.

And yet, these are the very moments where clarity trumps compassion. My life is not about enabling people who caused harm to others but rather about holding them accountable for their actions. It's not always comfortable, but it's essential because there are so few who are willing to sacrifice their likability to stop pain being caused in others.

I pressed, "You do realize that this behavior can traumatize others?"

His crying stopped, and he got up in anger. I was not buying his "act of innocence," and he was not getting the enabling energy he hoped for. One of the ladies in the group went to console him, so his ploy as the victim did not fail completely.

Unfortunately, Sean's behavior is not isolated. The attraction to creating intimacy and utilizing it as a pickup opportunity is widespread. Master manipulators can also use connection to get money or power.

This all guides me to another quote from my mentor: "Your intentions do not change the consequences of your actions." If we intend to create a warm and loving experience but it's hijacked by blind sexual desires, we are responsible for the results of our actions, even if our intentions were good.

Lesson: Beware of people who use connection to manipulate.

Exercise 28: Geiger Counter

This chapter was all about the parts of connection that are honestly
a bit scary: the times when a cold caller tries to manipulate you
into buying something, a friend tries to push you into something
uncomfortable, or a charismatic guru hijacks your good judgment.
To sense how easily this can be done, we are going to do the Geiger
Counter exercise. In this exercise, you will be presented with
situations where people are trying to manipulate you. Read each
sentence and feel how far the Geiger counter in your gut reacts to it.

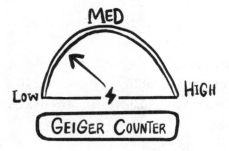

Cold caller says, "Do you want to save money on your electrical bill?"

Husband says, "If you really loved me, you wouldn't fight me on this."

Teacher says, "Love is all about giving. If you love me, then please show me through your donations."

Teacher touches a student in loving ways without consent and says, "If you are uncomfortable with that, there is some inner work that you still have to do."

Teacher says, "Until you really know connection, you will never be able to receive love. I can help you there."

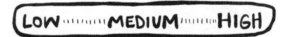

Family says, "If you renounce the church, we will not see you in the afterlife."

You may have felt the subtle and not so subtle ways that people use connection as a way to manipulate. It is something to be aware of, and yet, if we live in fear of it, we miss out on many opportunities for deeper connection. The lesson here is that if you feel someone pushing you in a direction under the guise of creating connection, trust your instinct. Either bring it forward or separate yourself. It may not be comfortable, but learning to trust this instinct is an important part of inviting connection into our lives.

CHAPTER 29

Loving from Afar

Although this book is about how to connect, it's a common trap to assume that connection is the goal in any relationship. If there is one thing that I'd like to scream from the mountaintops, it would be that you don't need connection. God forbid another belief has secretly worked its way into your system through this book. What I want to specify is that when connection exists, there is a higher likelihood that we will be in connection with ourselves and therefore others.

However, what happens when connection with another is not desirable? How do we deal with situations where we do not want to make a connection or the other does not want to make a connection with us?

My rules on this are simple, and they go back to the beginning chapters of this book. If the relationship does not have trust and respect, then I start there. I explore what is possible by not making too many assumptions and by investigating together where things might be off.

This all leads to one of the great challenges in life: How do we surrender—especially when it hurts? We do not get to control how another person interacts with us. That is their prerogative. We do not even get to blame them for their behavior. What we can do is decide for ourselves if we are getting what we want out of the relationship. That can be transactional in the form of money or more intimate in the form of meaningful interactions.

What we also do not get to do—and I want to stress this—is judge another for not meeting us in the way we'd like to be met. And I'd take a further step and say that if we are judging another for their lack of "connection," then we are falling into the trap of arrogance, thinking that our way is better. I've seen it happen on many occasions, and I have unfortunately fallen into the trap myself.

As I've made clear throughout this book, my wife and I have different interests. For the first few years of our relationship, I wanted her to attend self-development courses with me. I judged her for her lack of interest. I thought that she was missing out on the chance for "real intimacy."

I was unable to be vulnerable in our relationship, so I pushed her to go to a group so we could do it in public. In retrospect, I cringe at the thought that I was asking her to be vulnerable without ever being vulnerable myself. The hard lesson that I learned was to either accept and love her for who she was or separate from her. I began to connect with her more vulnerably, and, not surprisingly, she met me there. No course required.

And yet there are people who have no interest in meeting us in connection. When we have an emotional connection or a long history with this person, it can be doubly painful. As we grow, the types of relationships we prefer change. How we want to interact with others evolves. We see that our present desire for connection cannot be met by our present company.

What we sometimes fail to see is that we are the ones who have made the decision to change. The people around us may have not. When we meet these same people and are no longer getting what we need from the contact, it's easy to blame the other—to say, "You are superficial," or, "I'm sick of you talking about other people." We are blaming them for not meeting our needs, but that is not their responsibility; it is our own.

There are a handful of people in my life from whom I have chosen to separate. I don't blame them for this, nor do I seek understanding.

But I'm clear that the relationship no longer serves me. I'm witnessing a behavior that makes it undesirable to show up in my vulnerability.

One friendship jumps out when I think of this. I had a friend who, whenever I spoke, always turned the conversation back to himself. As if every life event were a competition. Typical conversations with him went like this:

Me: "Hey, I'm going to do a class next week."

Him: "Good for you. I've done five classes like that already for $10,000 a day. I was told it was the best course that person had ever done."

Or:

Me: "I'm writing a book that will come out by the end of the year."

Him: "I was thinking about writing a book, but books are out. It's a waste of time. I'm building a funnel. That's the smart move."

This individual professed to be all about connection, yet his inability to make peace with this deep insecurity turned into a behavior that I could no longer make space for. On the few occasions that I brought this forward vulnerably, it was met with a dismissive, condescending comment that further elevated his position as the "superior trainer."

After several such interactions, it was time to move on. If I had believed that connection was necessary, it would have been tough to separate. I would have tried over and over again and gotten stuck. Since there was no possibility for connection, believing there was would have been utterly exhausting. It would have turned into a codependent relationship. So I made peace with the fact that the conditions were not there for a relationship that I desired. There was no longer anything meaningful in it for me.

The important word I use here is "conditions." Instead of saying that a person caused the breakup, which makes it personal, I point out that the conditions are not there for a relationship in which I want to invest my time and energy.

In the story above, I saw that the trust was gone. I respected my friend for what he was endeavoring to achieve, but his consistent behavior over time showed that I could no longer trust that he would meet me in vulnerability. Instead, he turned my vulnerability into opportunities to gain leverage and take a position of superiority. It was a moment to say, "The conditions are not there for a healthy relationship at this time."

I certainly don't foreclose on the idea of reclaiming a relationship in the future. But connection is based on trust, and as I have said time and time again, if trust is lost in a relationship, then there is nothing to build on.

As you think of connection throughout this book, don't consider it a measuring stick by which to judge yourself or others. Rather, view it as a compass that helps you better understand yourself. By better understanding ourselves, we better understand the people in our lives.

And as I mentioned, it's not always possible. Sometimes the conditions are not there, and all we can do is move on and have compassion for the sadness that comes up. The journey of life is one of constant change. Many people will enter our lives for parts and leave in others. There is nothing wrong with this. Appreciate them for what they have brought you, and look at them with gratitude. The connection we seek with others evolves as we shift the connection within ourselves.

Lesson: Connection is not always possible or desirable.

Exercise 29: Present Conditions

This chapter brought forward a word that I use often in my coaching and mentoring: "conditions." This word encapsulates several important topics addressed in this book, including impersonal, possible no-match discussions, and saying no. To help you think about conditions in your own life, we will do the Present Conditions exercise. In this exercise, we list conditions with three checkboxes next to each to signify whether the condition in question is never a condition, sometimes a condition, or almost always a condition. Mark the box that is most true for you.

Statement	Never	Sometimes	Almost Always
I only get into relationships where I feel loved.			
I only spend time with people who bring me joy.			
I only enter relationships where I am being valued.			
I never put money before my well-being.			
When I am unhappy with someone I care about, I bring it forward.			
I never accept when someone says, "I am going to tell you something, but you can't tell anyone."			
I never remain silent when I see someone hurt another, even if it's unintentional.			

If you reflect on your answers, you'll possibly see sentences you marked "never" or "sometimes." This is not a contest, so those answers are not meant to be judged. The questions you can reflect upon are, "If I could answer 'almost always' to the questions above, how would my life change? What are the things or people that I may have to say goodbye to if I set those conditions for my life? How comfortable am I simply saying, 'The conditions are not here for a relationship I want to be in'?"

Living with strong conditions can be challenging. Living without strong conditions can be even harder. We bring conditions into our lives not to make them more difficult but rather to make peace with how we really want to live.

CHAPTER 30

Knowing When to Disconnect

As I write this book, a friend of mine is going through a divorce. We met five years ago, and since then I have been supporting him and, to a lesser degree, his wife. Although they loved each other deeply, their relationship was volatile. There were triggers and patterns on both sides that created ongoing conflict that never seemed to be resolved.

What I saw was a deep desire to make it work but a mismatch in what they were looking for in their relationship. At the core, they each wanted to be seen and heard, but a dynamic from the past continued to come back. They finally decided to call it quits. The decision was not filled with the sound and fury their arguments once had. It signified a clear resolve that their journeys were not meant to continue with one another. There was love, acceptance, and surrender to an uncertain future.

My friend is now clear on what he wants from his relationships, and I have never seen him more connected in his interactions. He made this journey to connect with his wife, but in the end, he connected with himself, and together they decided to end it.

The lesson here is this: The goal of improving our interactions is not to be together or stay together with another. Rather, it is to get closer to ourselves so that we can then see what is meant to be. Just because I *can* be with you does not mean that we are *meant* to be together.

In the previous chapter, we discussed knowing when the conditions do not exist to make a meaningful connection. Now I want to take this even further and discuss cases where this is stronger, more painful, more consequential. For example, divorce, separating from a business partner, or choosing to stop contact with a parent.

Taking responsibility for how we interact with others can be a challenging journey. We do not take this journey for the other. When I was younger, I saw that the common element in all my failed relationships was me. That was my reason to change. If I had wanted to change so that I could get the other person to be someone else, then that would have led to resentment. If we behave a certain way in the expectation that another will behave differently, we are setting ourselves up for failure.

Which brings me to the point of this chapter. When we begin breaking a negative reinforcing loop with a partner, we take away something in the dynamic between us. Even in an unhealthy dynamic, people get accustomed to a way of interacting. Each person is triggered by the other, and the interaction digresses to tension, resentment, or a fight. This might also be when the codependency kicks in.

When we make the decision to start improving our relations, there is a period of rebalance in our relationships. Although we are endeavoring to improve things with the people around us, they may not have made that decision. Or maybe they have, but the speed at which they are changing is not enough for our comfort.

Herein lies one of the hardest parts of anyone's personal journey. As we begin to evolve out of blame, shame, and negotiating behavior that has kept us stuck, what we are looking for in our relationships may also change. Even if we can manage the relationship better because we have the tools, it does not mean that we will still be together with the person we began this journey with.

It may seem strange. If we're better at interacting, wouldn't we stay with the person we're with now? The answer to that question is yes and no. Yes, we now have the tools to interact more meaningfully; and no, we may realize that we want more.

Couples are often so busy trying to make their relationship work that they never stop to ask the question, "Is this the person I want to make it work with?" Once we've raised our awareness of how to better interact in relationships, this becomes a very real question. In my experience, if a couple grows through this process together, there is a higher likelihood that the answer to that question is a resounding yes. If only one partner takes this journey, it's less likely.

Once a person no longer interacts from fear and anger, they begin to desire more meaningful contact. If that contact cannot be made with their current partner, then they will often find it outside of the relationship. Not necessarily with another partner, but possibly with other groups that share the intimacy they are missing in their current relationship. To clarify, it is not that their relationships don't have some intimacy. But how do we deal with one another when times get tough? How do we support each other through our challenges? How do we hold one another during our greatest losses and achievements?

When we begin to take responsibility for ourselves, we will change. And in that change, we become someone different, with different needs and wants. As painful as it is, there are times when the most harmonious path, both for ourselves and others, is actually to disconnect from those around us.

Which all leads to my final point. We have so many moments in life where we can choose what path we want to follow. When we begin to follow the path inward to find connection within ourselves, we are like astronauts discovering a new world. As President Kennedy said, "We choose to go to the moon in this decade and do the other things, not because they are easy, but because they are hard, because that goal will serve to organize and measure the best of our energies and skills."

I invite you to make your own moon landing. And as I have mentioned several times in this book, success lies not in the outcome but in the act of trying. I love you, and thank you for spending these hours with me as we dance along this journey together.

✳ ✳ ✳

Exercise 30: Anchoring the Future

As a final lesson, I'd like to ask you to reflect on the book and create some anchors for yourself. What are the things that you will do differently based on what you learned in this book? The more specific you are, the easier it will be to hold true to them in the future. I will start with a few:

- I will be more loving to myself when I am struggling in my relationships.
- I will pause when I hear myself judging as I speak.
- I will not push down my feelings when they arise.

Holding true to new life patterns takes a lot of determination and willpower. Use the items that you have written above as an anchor for your future. When you feel yourself going astray, slow down, take a breath, and try again. One of the greatest misconceptions of the word "success" is that it is a state reached at the end of a journey. Nothing could be further from the truth. Success is waking up day after day and dedicating to being a better person than we were the day before.

CLOSING

I have longed for connection all of my life. When my mother died when I was eighteen years old and my father rejected me, I felt deep loneliness. The kind of loneliness that makes you wonder if life is worth living. I spent years avoiding connection so that I did not need to feel the depth of my losses. Touching intimacy reminded me over and over again of what I had lost with my mother's death. Yet with time and care, I saw that the only thing that gave my life meaning was in fact the one thing I had avoided: connection.

As I learned how to invite people into my life, I made many mistakes along the way. I was sometimes overzealous and other times overprotective. I learned that in the end, there were no real mistakes. Everything that happened was necessary in order to learn the lessons that have brought me here today. I laugh when anyone asks for my credentials. I smile and say, "I have made so many mistakes in my life that I have a really good idea of what doesn't work."

As you move forward in your journey, it is important to treat yourself with love and care. This is a marathon, not a sprint. People will come in and out of your life. There will be moments when you think you're alone. There will be times when you feel there is no hope. All of this is part of the journey to healing and building connection with yourself and then with others.

In an interview, Tom Hanks was asked, "If you could go back to your younger self, what piece of advice would you give yourself?"

His answer was both beautiful and inspiring. He said, "I wish I had known that this too shall pass. You feel bad right now. You feel pissed off and angry. This too shall pass. You feel great. You feel like you know all the answers. You feel that everybody finally gets you. This too shall pass."

There is no goal. There is just a constant opportunity to make the most of this moment. Connection makes that possible.

I love you. These are not just words. I truly feel this as I write. I can't describe how good that feels to simultaneously write and feel. I spent the majority of my life saying those words and separating from their meaning. In reconnecting back to that deep sense of love, I rediscovered connection.

I hope that our time together has helped you connect with yourself and those you care about.

EXERCISE ANSWERS

Exercise 6: Check It Out

	Observation	Expectation
It is normal to get married after dating.		X
There are 365 days in a year.	X	
Kids should be out of the house by twenty-one years old.		X
She will leave the house at twenty-one years old.		X
It's important to get good grades in school.		X
One-night stands are wrong.		X
Music soothes the soul.		X
I listen to soul music.	X	
People should be able to speak a second language.		X
It will be seventy degrees tomorrow.		X
It is seventy degrees now.	X	
A family house should have a garden.		X
We are going to Spain next month.		X
When the floor is dirty, mice will come.		X
I sing in front of crowds.	X	
The medicine will cure the cold.		X
Twenty percent of the population speaks Spanish.	X	
He was five minutes late to the meeting.	X	
Meetings should start on time.		X

Exercise 7: Assume Away

"You are trying too hard."
"What do you mean by 'too'?"
"How do you see that?"
"Where do you experience that?"

"I'm getting frustrated with you."
"How?"
"What am I doing to frustrate you?"
"What do you mean by 'frustrated'?"

"The class needs to change."
"What do you think needs to change?"
"What do you see?"
"What do you mean by 'change'?"
"Change how?"

"The house is dirty!"
"How?"
"What's dirty?"
"What do you mean by 'dirty'?"
"Dirty how?"

Exercise 9: Truth or Dare

"This is a stupid idea."
"How do you see it as stupid?"
"What do you mean?"
"How do you see that?"
"Stupid how?"

"What's your problem?"
"What do you mean?"
"What problem do you see?"
"Problem?"

"How could you say that?"
"What are you referring to?"
"Say what?"
"What is that?"

"You are not that smart."
"How do you mean?"
"What do you see?"
"What gives you that impression?"

"Mainstream media is so biased."
"What do you see?"
"What does mainstream mean to you?"
"How do you see it biased?"

"Aliens do exist. It's a fact."
"How do you know?"
"What's your experience with this?"
"How did you get into this?"

Exercise 10: Lens of Love

Judgment	Love
He is so disrespectful.	He does not appear to see the consequences of his actions.
She is a liar.	She has said things many times that do not match what I see as reality.

He is lazy.	He is comfortable sitting around all day. That's not easy for me.
I don't like him.	I see that I am not comfortable around him.
She is a drama queen.	I see that I get triggered when she speaks.
They are impolite.	They have a way of acting which does not make me feel comfortable.
What a jerk.	He is comfortable being so direct that it can cause people to leave.

Exercise 13: Label You

Label	Personal	Impersonal
They are anti-vaxxers.	They are brainwashed.	They have different beliefs than I do.
They are one-percenters.	They are greedy.	They are extremely wealthy.
He's uneducated.	He is not smart.	He did not go to school.
He's unprofessional.	He is crass.	He speaks freely.
She's shallow.	She is superficial.	She doesn't share vulnerably.

Exercise 14: Five Steps Down

Level 1: "You're screwing up your life."
Level 2: "I'm frustrated with you."
Level 3: "What you are doing makes me nervous."
Level 4: "I'm uncomfortable with what I see."
Level 5: "I'm scared."

Level 1: "Your partner is terrible."
Level 2: "Your partner needs to change."

Level 3: "I don't like how your partner is treating you."
Level 4: "I think you need to do something."
Level 5: "I'm worried."

Level 1: "You are totally unreliable."
Level 2: "I don't like your behavior."
Level 3: "You need to think about how you are living."
Level 4: "I am having trouble planning with you."
Level 5: "I miss seeing you."

Level 1: "You are lazy."
Level 2: "You are screwing up your life."
Level 3: "I don't like your attitude."
Level 4: "I'm worried for you."
Level 5: "I feel helpless."

Exercise 17: Sort It Out

Group 1:
"I've been struggling, and I'd like to discuss our relationship."
"I feel like there are things we can discuss to improve our relations."
"I'd love to talk about how we can get things flowing between us again."

Group 2:
"Due to staff changes, we are here to discuss some important changes."
"This meeting will give us a chance to begin planning the transition."
"I hope that by the end everyone will feel better about where we are heading."

Group 3:

"I saw what you published online today, and I was hoping to talk with you."

"If you are free for lunch tomorrow, I would love to discuss what you plan to do in the future."

"It would be great to see if there is a chance that we could find some overlaps in our activities."

Exercise 21: Flip the Script

"Is this a good book?"
"How is the book?"

"Are you well?"
"How are you?"

"Can you finish on time?"
"When do you think you'll finish?"

"Is it possible for you to do it?"
"How do you feel about doing it?"

"Are you looking forward to the trip?"
"What are you looking forward to on the trip?"

"Can we see each other next week?"
"How is your schedule next week?"

Exercise 22: Dig Deeper

"The family is living beyond its means."
"Beyond?"

"He is too logical."
"How too?"

"They don't make a good couple."
"What do you mean by 'don't'?"

"The project is bound to fail."
"Fail how?"

Exercise 26: Turn It Around

Situation 1: You mistakenly press send on an email to a person with embarrassing information about them in it.

> d) I just sent you a stupid email. I wrote some things in it about you, and I realize now that was not right or fair. I'd be grateful if you'd be open to discussing it.

Situation 2: A customer that you have been working with for years tells you that they are canceling the contract and going to the competition.

> b) I completely understand that you have reasons to leave us. Would you be open to getting on a call so that I can better understand what we might be able to improve in the future?

Situation 3: In the middle of an intense argument with a friend, you lose your cool and say something that hurts them deeply.

> c) I'm so sorry I hurt you. I was feeling so much pain, and I lashed out. I really wanted to hurt you because I felt like you were hurting me, and that was not right.

Exercise 27: The Mirror Has Two Faces

Facing Negative	Facing Positive
You are not doing what we agreed to.	I'd love it if we could find something that we both can agree to. It will make it easier for me and I hope you.
You are talking nonsense.	Please help me understand what you are trying to say. I'm just not getting it.

NOTES

1   Molenberghs, Pascal and Louis, Winnifred R. "Insights From fMRI Studies Into Ingroup Bias." 2018. https://www.frontiersin.org/articles/10.3389/fpsyg.2018.01868/full.

2   Hobson, Nicholas M. and Inzlicht, Michael. *Social Cognitive and Affective Neuroscience*, Volume 11, Issue 11, November 2016, Pages 1698–1706, https://doi.org/10.1093/scan/nsw082.

3   Whitehead, Nadia. "People would rather be electrically shocked than left alone with their thoughts." *Science Magazine*. July 3, 2014. https://www.sciencemag.org/news/2014/07/people-would-rather-be-electrically-shocked-left-alone-their-thoughts

4   Korisky, Adi; Eisenberger, Naomi I.; Nevat, Michael; Weissman-Fogel, Irit; and Shamay-Tsoory, Simone G. "A dual-brain approach for understanding the neuralmechanisms that underlie the comforting effects of social touch." *ScienceDirect*. March 11, 2020.

Printed in the USA
CPSIA information can be obtained
at www.ICGtesting.com
JSHW081829021023
49226JS00003B/23